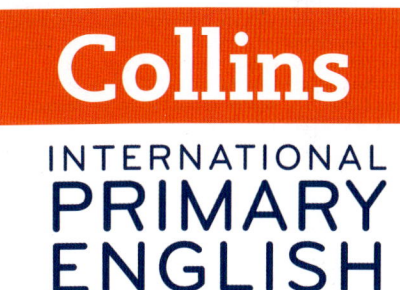

Collins
INTERNATIONAL PRIMARY ENGLISH

Student's Book 3

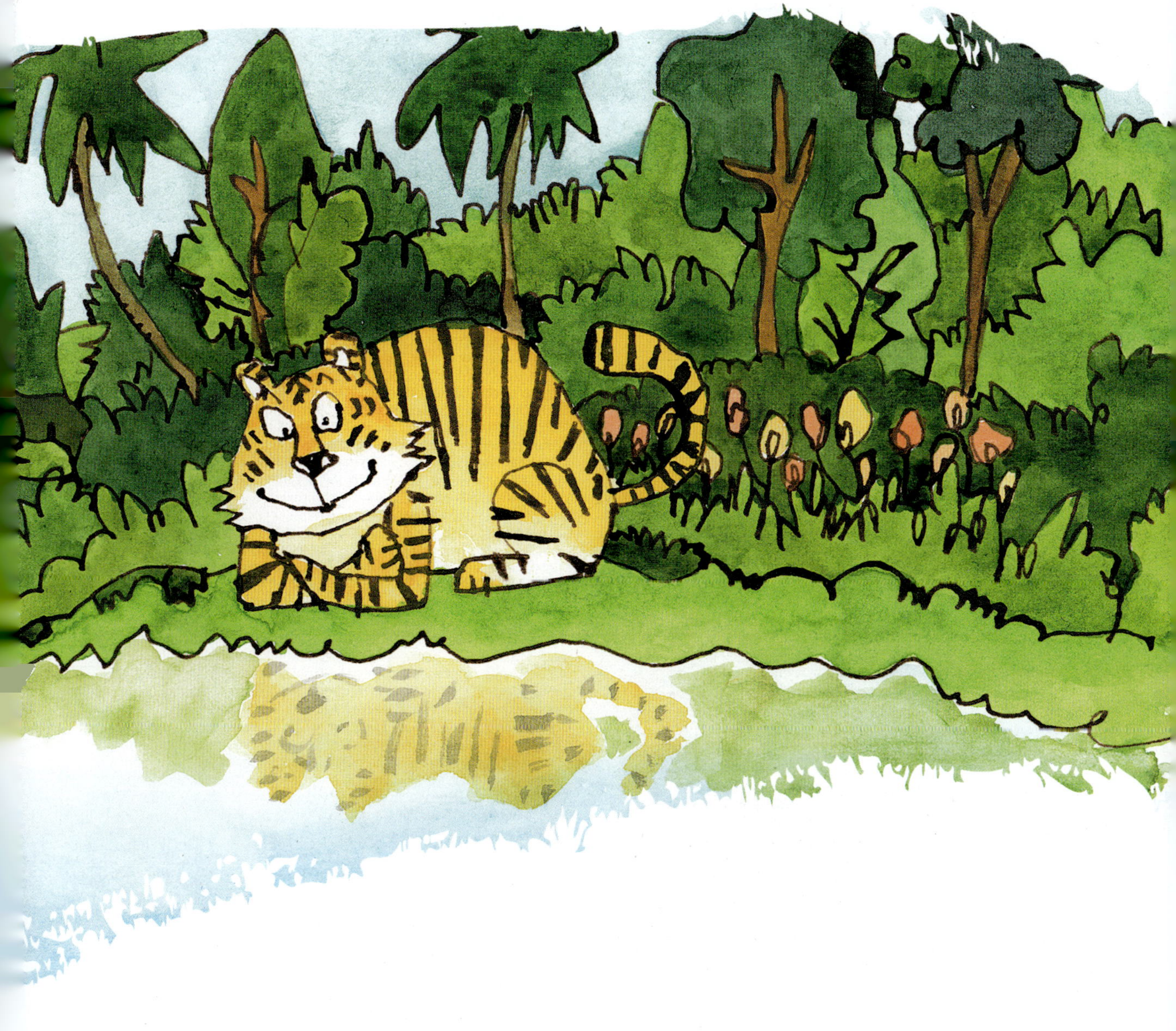

William Collins' dream of knowledge for all began with the publication of his first book in 1819. A self-educated mill worker, he not only enriched millions of lives, but also founded a flourishing publishing house. Today, staying true to this spirit, Collins books are packed with inspiration, innovation and practical expertise. They place you at the centre of a world of possibility and give you exactly what you need to explore it.

Collins. Freedom to teach.

Published by Collins
An imprint of HarperCollins*Publishers*
The News Building
1 London Bridge Street
London SE1 9GF

HarperCollinsPublishers
Macken House, 39/40 Mayor Street Upper,
Dublin 1, D01 C9W8, Ireland

Browse the complete Collins catalogue at
www.collins.co.uk

© HarperCollins*Publishers* Limited 2021

10 9 8 7

ISBN 978-0-00-836765-7

All rights reserved. No part of this publication may be reproduced, stored in a retrieval system, or transmitted in any form by any means, electronic, mechanical, photocopying, recording or otherwise, without the prior written permission of the Publisher or a licence permitting restricted copying in the United Kingdom issued by the Copyright Licensing Agency Ltd, 5th Floor, Shackleton House, 4 Battle Bridge Lane, London SE1 2HX.

British Library Cataloguing-in-Publication Data
A catalogue record for this publication is available from the British Library.

Author: Daphne Paizee
Series editor: Daphne Paizee
Publisher: Elaine Higgleton
Product developer: Natasha Paul
Project manager: Karen Williams
Development editor: Sonya Newland
Copyeditor: Karen Williams
Proofreader: Catherine Dakin
Cover designer: Gordon MacGilp
Cover illustrator: Satoshi Kitamura
Internal designer and typesetter: Ken Vail Graphic Design Ltd.
Text permissions researcher: Rachel Thorne
Image permissions researcher: Alison Prior
Illustrators: Ken Vail Graphic Design Ltd., Advocate Art, Beehive Illustration and QBS Learning
Production controller: Lyndsey Rogers
Printed in India by Multivista Global Pvt.Ltd.

Third-party websites, publications and resources referred to in this publication have not been endorsed by Cambridge Assessment International Education.

With thanks to the following teachers and schools for reviewing materials in development: Amanda DuPratt, Shreyaa Dutta Gupta, Sharmila Majumdar, Sushmita Ray and Sukanya Singhal, Calcutta International School; Akash Raut, DSB International School, Mumbai; Melissa Brobst, International School of Budapest; Shalini Reddy, Manthan International School; Taman Rama Intercultural School.

Text acknowledgements
The publishers gratefully acknowledge the permissions granted to reproduce copyright material in the book. Every effort has been made to contact the holders of copyright material, but if any have been inadvertently overlooked, the Publisher will be pleased to make the necessary arrangements at the first opportunity.

Cover illustration: *Tiger Dead! Tiger Dead!* Reprinted by permission of HarperCollins*Publishers* Ltd © 2009 Grace Nichols and John Agard, illustrated by Satoshi Kitamura.

The Rescue Reprinted by permission of HarperCollins*Publishers* Ltd © 2013 Alan Durant, illustrated by Stave James; *Bugs!* Reprinted by permission of HarperCollins*Publishers* Ltd © 2010 Sam McBratney, illustrated by Eric Smith; *Harry the Clever Spider* Reprinted by permission of HarperCollins*Publishers* Ltd © 2005 Julia Jarman, illustrated by Charlie Fowkes; *Why Can't Humans Fly?* Reprinted by permission of HarperCollins*Publishers* Ltd © 2012 Sarah Fleming, illustrated by Wes Lowe; *Africa's Big Three* Reprinted by permission of HarperCollins*Publishers* Ltd © 2006 Jonathan and Angela Scott; *Let's Go To Mars!* Reprinted by permission of HarperCollins*Publishers* Ltd © 2005 Janice Marriott, illustrated by Mark Ruffle; *The Brave Baby* Reprinted by permission of HarperCollins*Publishers* Ltd © 2004 Malachy Doyle, illustrated by Richard Johnson; *Fossils* Reprinted by permission of HarperCollins*Publishers* Ltd © 2010 Dr Andrew Ross; *Motocross* Reprinted by permission of HarperCollins*Publishers* Ltd © 2013 Adrian Bradbury; *The Journey of Humpback Whales* Reprinted by permission of HarperCollins*Publishers* Ltd © 2012 Andy Belcher; *Captain Scott: Journey to the South Pole* Reprinted by permission of HarperCollins*Publishers* Ltd © 2012 Adrian Bradbury, illustrated by Kate Evans and Bob Moulder; *Chicken Licken* Reprinted by permission of HarperCollins*Publishers* Ltd © 2007 Jeremy Strong, illustrated by Tony Blundell; *The Stone Cutter* Reprinted by permission of HarperCollins*Publishers* Ltd © 2005 Sean Taylor, illustrated by Serena Curmi; *The Titanic* Reprinted by permission of HarperCollins*Publishers* Ltd © 2012 Anna Claybourne.

We are grateful to the following for permission to reproduce copyright material:

Extracts on pp.3435, 36 from *Wild Things: Leopard Trail* by Elizabeth Laird, first published by Macmillan Children's Books, an imprint of Pan Macmillan, 1999, copyright © Elizabeth Laird, 1999. Reproduced by permission of Macmillan Publishers International Limited; An extract on p.39 from 'The Shepherd Boy at School' by Elizabeth Laird from *When the World Began, Stories Collected in Ethiopia*, Oxford University Press, 2001. Reproduced with permission of the Licensor through PLSclear; The poems on pp.85, 86 'Riddle' by Judith Nicholls, published in *Storm's Eye*, Oxford University Press, 1994, copyright © Judith Nicholls 1994; and 'Teacher said …' by Judith Nicholls, published in *Magic Mirror*, Faber & Faber, 1985, copyright © Judith Nicholls 1985. Reprinted by permission of the author; The poem on p.89 'Ice Cream and Fizzy Lemonade' by Stanley Cook, published in *Woods Beyond a Cornfield: Collected Poems by Stanley Cook*, Smith|doorstop, 1995. Reproduced with permission from The Poetry Business; The poem on p.90 'Night Songs' by Lynn Joseph, from *Coconut Kind of Day: Island Poems* by Lynn Joseph, Puffin Books, 1992. Reproduced with kind permission of the author; The poem on p.90 'Hurricane' from *Earth Magic* by Dionne Brand and illustrations by Eugenie Fernandes, text copyright © 1979, 2006 Dionne Brand. Reproduced by permission of Kids Can Press Ltd., Toronto, Canada; and the poem on p.91 "Fishes' Evening Song' by Dahlov Ipcar, copyright © 1967 by Dahlov Ipcar, © 2019 Robert Ipcar. Reprinted with permission of McIntosh & Otis, Inc.

In some instances we have been unable to trace the owners of copyright material, and we would appreciate any information that would enable us to do so.

Photo acknowledgements
The publishers wish to thank the following for permission to reproduce photographs. Every effort has been made to trace copyright holders and to obtain their permission for the use of copyright materials. The publishers will gladly receive any information enabling them to rectify any error or omission at the first opportunity.

(t = top, c = centre, b = bottom, r = right, l = left)

p1a potowizard/Shutterstock, p1b Steve Photography/Shutterstock, p1c Lafoto/Shutterstock, p1d Keren Su/Getty Images, p1e Chuck Wagner/Shutterstock, p1f Kotenko Oleksandr/Shutterstock, p5tl Rob Marmion/Shutterstock, p5tc Volt Collection/Shutterstock, p5tr Alexzel/Shutterstock, p9bl Ian Nellist/Alamy Stock Photo, p9r Joseph Sohm/Shutterstock, p10 Asianet-Pakistan/Shutterstock, p11 Kirill Neiezhmakov/Shutterstock, p14 Andrey_Popov/Shutterstock, p15 REDPIXEL.PL/Shutterstock, p24t Irin-k/Shutterstock, p24c Valentina Proskurina/Shutterstock, p24b Mathagraphics/ Shutterstock, p25 Carroteater/Shutterstock, p26 Matteo photos/Shutterstock, p27 Jorge Salcedo/Shutterstock, p28tr ImageDepotPro/iStockphoto.com, p28cr (rhino) Jonathan and Angela Scott/Getty Images, p28cr (hippo) Jonathan And Angela/Getty Images, p28br maximimages/Alamy Stock Photo, p28br Imago/ ActionPlus, p29 Amy Johansson/Shutterstock, p30 ChrisNoe/Shutterstock, p31 Hintau Aliaksei/Shutterstock, p34 Ondrej Prosicky/Shutterstock, p40 Ostill/Shutterstock, p41 Mark Carwardine/NaturePL.com, p42cl Mike Parry/Getty Images, p42tl Westend61/Shutterstock, p42cr, p42bl Flip Nicklin/Getty Images, p43t Christopher Swann/Science Photo Library, p43c Daniel Cox/Oxford Scientific/Getty Images, p43b David Tipling/Photographer's Choice/Getty Images, p45 Tierfotoagentur/ Alamy Stock Photo, p46t AndreAnita/Shutterstock, p46b Sekar B/Shutterstock, p47 Monkey Business Images/Shutterstock, p48 Popperfoto/Getty Images, p49t Time Life Pictures/Mansell/Getty Images, p49b The Print Collector/Alamy Stock Photo, p50 INTERFOTO/ Alamy Stock Photo, p57tl Maridav /Shutterstock, p57tr Paul looyen/Shutterstock, p57bl Frank Fichtmueller/Shutterstock, p57br Rostilav Stefanek/Shutterstock, p65bl domnistsky/Shutterstock, p65br Alexander Tolstykh/Shutterstock, p75 Courtesy Everett Collection/Rex Features, p76cl World History Archive/Alamy, p76br Public Domain/Olympic and Titanic White Star Line, p77tr, cl World History Archive/Alamy Stock Photo, p77br Library of Congress/Wikimedia Commons, p79 North Wind Picture Archives/Alamy Stock Photo, p80 Denis Burdin/Shutterstock, p81 Pictorial Press/Alamy Stock Photo, p83 Oleksandr Kalinichneko/Shutterstock, p89 noBorders-Brayden Howie/Shutterstock, p92 Wavebreakmedia/Shutterstock.

This book contains FSC™ certified paper and other controlled sources to ensure responsible forest management.

For more information visit: www.harpercollins.co.uk/green

Contents

How to use this book

1 **Danger!** page 1

2 **Staying in touch** page 11

3 **Bugs** page 20

4 **A good read** page 28

5 **Amazing journeys** page 40

6 **Myths and legends** page 52

7 **On stage** page 63

8 **Amazing ships** page 75

9 **Sights, sounds and feelings** page 84

To the teacher

How to use this book

- **Key texts and images**
  The texts in Stage 3 provide a wide variety of different genres for learners to enjoy. The colourful illustrations provide enjoyment as well as essential support for learners as they learn to read. Learners are introduced to stories by published authors and a variety of illustration styles.

- **Remember boxes**
  These are used to remind learners to do things that they have already learned, such as the correct use of punctuation marks.

  Remember!
  In group talk, remember to share your own ideas and listen politely to other people's.

- **Word book**
  These are used throughout this course. Word books allow learners to compile their own personal dictionaries which they can refer to in their writing activities. They also help learners to develop dictionary skills.

  Word book
  Write interesting adjectives in your Word book. Use them in your own writing.

- **Thinking time**
  These occur at the end of each unit in the Student's Book. Learners are encouraged to reflect on what they have read, listened to, discussed and learned.

  Thinking time
  - How did you work out the meanings of unfamiliar words you read in this unit?
  - Look at the words you have written in your Word book. Have you used any of them in your writing?

1 Danger!

Listening and speaking

GROUP WORK. Look at the pictures. Talk about any dangers you can see.

Reading and writing

1. Copy the sentences below. Underline the nouns. Circle the adjectives.

   a The workers were wearing hard hats.
   b There was a huge fire on the mountain.
   c A fierce thunderstorm struck the boat.
   d There were big cars and small cars in the street.
   e The metal ladder was against the wall of the house.
   f The terrified boy was clinging to a rock on the mountain.

2. Choose four of the pictures. Write new sentences to describe the pictures. Use an adjective in each sentence.

Reading and speaking

1 Read the title and look at the pictures in the story below.

   a Who are the characters in this story?
   b What is the setting for this story? (Where does it happen?) What do you think the theme is?
   c What do you think this story is about?

2 Now read the story silently to yourself.

> **Remember!**
> If you are not sure how to read a word, divide it into syllables. For example: res/cue, har/ness.

> **Adventure stories**
> Adventure stories have:
> - heroic characters.
> - an unusual or dangerous setting.
> - a dramatic plot.

The Rescue
by Alan Durant

"Hold on, Tom!" a voice shouted from above me. But I didn't know how long I could hold on. "Help is on the way!" It was Alex, my best friend, who was shouting.

We'd been having such a great time. How could it all have gone so wrong?

It was a sunny day. Alex and I had decided to take a walk along the cliff top. The view was amazing from up there. I was looking over the edge of the cliff when my foot slipped from under me.

"Agh!" I cried in panic, as the ground suddenly fell away.

Terrified, I slid down the rock face. Somehow, I managed to grab hold of a narrow ledge.

I was clinging on to the rock, but I was starting to get cramp in my hands. I could feel my fingers slipping – I was losing my grip.

"Hold on, Tom!" Alex called again. "Help won't be long."

But how long could I hold on? Soon I would drop on to the rocks below.

Some gulls flew by me. If only I had wings, I thought. My legs dangled in the air, and I felt faint and dizzy. I was so tired. "Give up, let go," said a soft voice inside my head.

But there was another voice. It said, "Keep holding on. You must fight to save yourself."

> **Remember!**
> If you are not sure what a word means, read the whole sentence again. Does that help you work out the tricky word?

I was in pain from head to toe. I wouldn't look down and I couldn't look up.

I stared at the sheer rock in front of me. I willed myself to be strong. But it was no use. It was so hot and I was getting weak. I was going to fall. I was going to die.

And then I heard it. First there was a hum in the air, then a throb and a whirr. I couldn't see anything but the noise was getting louder, closer.

I could picture blades spinning round and round. It was so loud that my ears hurt.

A man in a harness banged against the rock beside me. He inched towards me, swinging on a rope.

"Almost there," he said. He put a belt round my waist. Then he pulled it tight. "Now, let go!" he shouted.

I still held on. What if my mind was playing tricks on me? What if I fell?

"Let go!" the man called once more – and this time I did.

For a moment, I was treading air. I couldn't breathe. I flapped my arms. My head rolled. Then I smiled as I saw I was going up, not down. I was rising towards the helicopter. I could see Alex on the cliff, and I waved and grinned. I was safe.

I'd been rescued.

Reading and speaking

1 **PAIR WORK. Answer the questions below.**

a What had Tom been doing at the beginning of the story?
b Why was he there?
c What did Tom hold on to?
d What noise did Tom hear that made his ears hurt?
e Who rescued Tom?
f How was Tom rescued?

2 **GROUP WORK. Talk about the questions below.**

a How did Tom feel while he waited to be rescued?
b Who do you think called the rescue helicopter?
c Do you think Tom was lucky to be rescued?
d What would you do if you were out with your friend and your friend had an accident?
e Did you enjoy the story? Why or why not?

3 **PAIR WORK. Read the story aloud.**

Remember!
Read the direct speech with lots of expression. Think how the character feels.

Reading and writing

Tom is the main character in the story *The Rescue*.

1 **PAIR WORK. Answer the questions below about Tom.**

a How do you think Tom feels as he waits for help?
b What sorts of activities do you think Tom enjoys?
c Which of these adjectives could you use to describe Tom?

> brave   sad   terrified   crazy
> silly   unhappy   scared

❷ **PAIR WORK. Look at the pictures. Talk about each character.**

❸ **Write a paragraph about one of the characters in the pictures. Describe what they look like, how they feel and what they like to do.**

a

b

c

Word book

Write interesting adjectives in your Word book. Use them in your own writing.

Using verbs

Copy the sentences below. Underline the verb in each sentence.

a I cried in panic.
b I slid down the rock face.
c I grabbed hold of a narrow ledge.
d I was clinging on to the rock
e Some gulls flew by me.
f My legs dangled in the air.
g I felt faint and dizzy.
h I was so tired.

Verbs

All sentences have verbs. Verbs describe actions. For example:

I **slipped** on a rock.
He **put** a belt round my waist.
I **was rising** towards the helicopter.

Words like 'have', 'has', 'am', 'is', 'are', 'was' and 'were' are also verbs. For example:

I **was** in pain from head to toe.
You **are** safe now. I **have** a good friend.

Remember!

Verbs have different forms. We use different forms to describe when an action happens. For example:

I **am** tired. Last night I **was** tired.
'Am' and 'was' are both forms of the verb 'to be'.
I **am slipping**. I **slipped**.
'Am slipping' and 'slipped' are both forms of the verb 'to slip'.

Listening and speaking

GROUP WORK. Read the verbs from the story.
Choose one verb and role-play the action it describes.
Your group must guess which word it is.

> stare   grin   dangle   tread (air)
> cling   slip   spin   flap

Spelling

Verbs with –ing

Sometimes we add the suffix –ing to a verb.
Examples:
look: I was **looking** over the edge of the cliff.
cling: I was **clinging** on to the rock.

Copy the sentences below. Complete the verbs with –ing.

a He was tell _____ me to hold on.
b I was go _____ to fall.
c I was get _____ weak.
d The man was swing _____ towards me on a rope.
e My mind was play _____ tricks on me.
f I was tread _____ air.

Word book

Write tricky words in your Word book. This will help you to remember how to spell them.

Remember!

Some words are irregular, which means that the spelling may be different. If the sound before the consonant is short, you need to double the last consonant.

get – getting   grin – grinning
slip – slipping

If the word ends with e, you drop the e before you add –ing.

rise – rising   smile – smiling

Vocabulary

1 GROUP WORK. Read the example and the explanation.

Example: There was a hum and a whirr in the air.
The words 'hum' and 'whirr' make the sentence interesting. The writer could just have said 'noise'.

2 Talk about which word in each of the sentences below makes it more interesting.

a The man inched towards me.
b The blades of the helicopter were spinning round and round.
c The view was amazing from up there!
d My legs dangled in the air.

3 Make the sentences below more interesting. Change the underlined word for one of the words in the box. Read your sentences aloud.

Example: "Hold on Tom!" <u>said</u> Alex.   "Hold on Tom!" <u>shouted</u> Alex.

| waved   grinned   terrible   called |

a I <u>moved</u> my arms.
b When I saw Alex and Stan I <u>smiled</u>.
c "Let's go!" <u>said</u> the pilot.
d There was a <u>bad</u> fire on the mountain last week.

Speaking

PAIR WORK. Retell the story of *The Rescue*. Use some of the interesting words you have talked about.

Writing

Imagine you are Tom's friend Alex. Write a description of what happened when you went out for a walk with Tom. Start by describing the setting.

Start like this: Yesterday afternoon Tom and I went for a walk. We walked …

Remember!

Describe the setting in your description. Say:
- where the actions happened.
- what sequence (order) they happened in.
- what the place looked like.

Using speech marks

In *The Rescue* the characters sometimes speak to each other. We call this dialogue. This text is written with speech marks before and after the words that the people say.

1 Read the dialogue below from the story. Then answer the questions.

> "Hold on, Tom!" a voice shouted from above me. But I didn't know how long I could hold on.
> "Help is on the way!" It was Alex, my best friend, who was shouting.

a Who spoke the words in speech marks?

b Who was the character speaking to?

c How did the character speak? Which word tells us how the character spoke?

Remember!

Make sure your handwriting is neat and clear.

Remember!

We use speech marks (" and ") to show the words that characters actually say in a story. These marks go at the beginning and end of the words. The rest of the story is narrative text, with no speech marks.

2 PAIR WORK. Look carefully at the speech marks in the sentences in question 1. Talk about how you can add speech marks to make the text below easier to read.

We are almost there, he said. He put the belt around my waist. Now, hold on tight.

Reading

Information texts
Newspaper articles give information about who, when, where, why and how something happened.

1 PAIR WORK. Look at the picture of the jet ski below. Describe the jet ski. Say what it looks like and where people use them.

2 Scan the newspaper text below about two fires. Then answer the questions. Look at the pictures carefully.

a Where was the first fire?
b Who did the firefighters rescue?
c What happened in the afternoon?
d How did they put out the fire?

A busy day for firefighters

Firefighters had a busy day yesterday. One team of firefighters was called out to sea early in the morning to put out a fire on a boat. Four people were trapped on the boat. The firefighters used jet skis and a fire boat to get to the small boat, which was in shallow water. They managed to rescue the fishermen and put out the fire.

In the afternoon a fire broke out in a large building in town. A large team of firefighters arrived in three fire engines. They put out the flames with powerful jets of water from hosepipes. The team worked hard and finally got the fire under control.

Listening and speaking

In the story *The Rescue*, Alex and the rescue pilot gave Tom some instructions.

"Hold on, Tom!"

"Let go, now!"

Imagine that there is a fire in your school. This is very dangerous, so you need to listen carefully to some instructions which your teacher will read to you.

1 **PAIR WORK. Repeat the instructions you heard to your partner.**

2 **PAIR WORK. Talk about why your teacher gave you the instructions. Give your opinions.**

   a Why did you have to walk quietly?
   b Why did you have to wait at the door?

3 **GROUP WORK. Imagine there is a flood near your house or school.**

Talk about what instructions you could give to your friends and family to help them to keep out of danger. The photograph below may give you some ideas.

Remember!

In group talk, remember to share your own ideas and listen politely to other people's.

Thinking time

- How did you work out the meanings of unfamiliar words you read in this unit?
- Look at the words you have written in your Word book. Have you used any of them in your writing?

2 Staying in touch

Reading and speaking

1 PAIR WORK. Look at the text below. Talk about the text.
Then answer the questions.

a What type of text is this?
b To whom is it addressed?
c Where is Mariam?
d How do you know where Mariam is?
e In what other way could she have sent this information?
f Is this a formal or an informal letter?

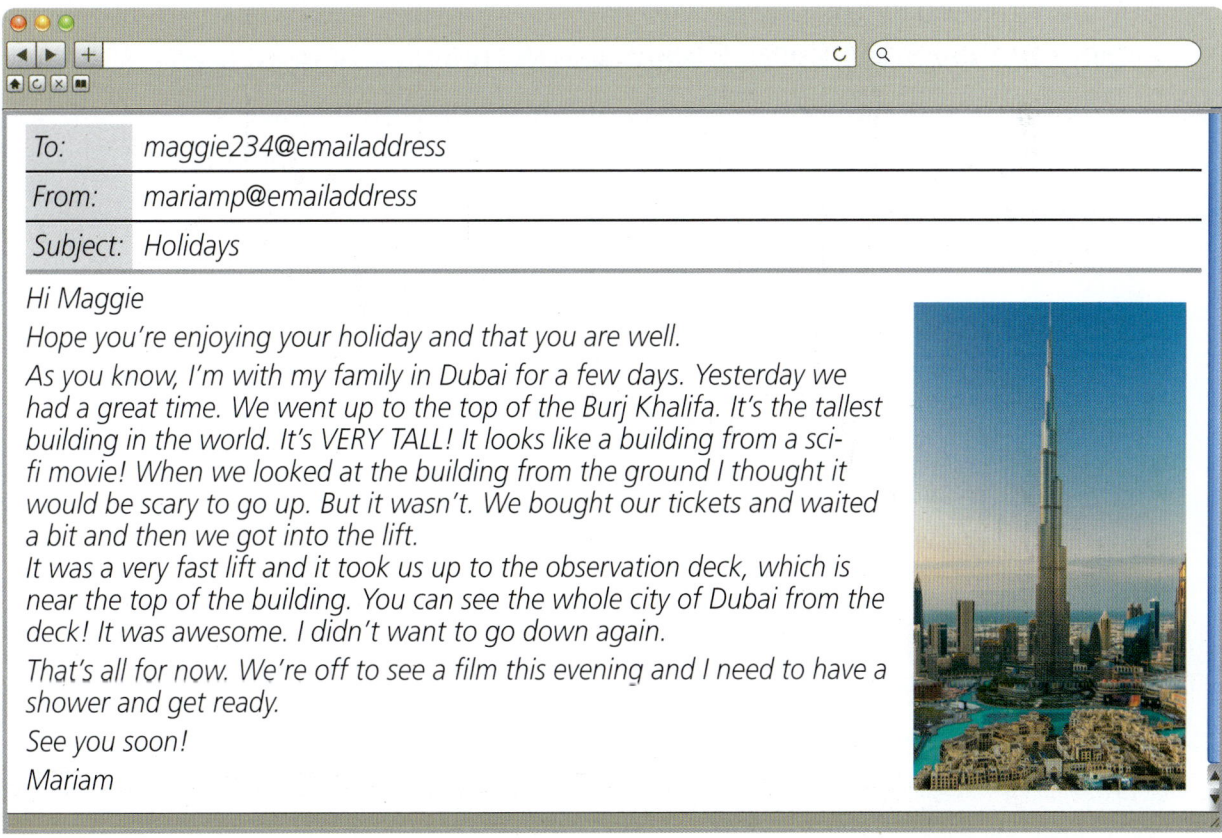

To: maggie234@emailaddress
From: mariamp@emailaddress
Subject: Holidays

Hi Maggie
Hope you're enjoying your holiday and that you are well.
As you know, I'm with my family in Dubai for a few days. Yesterday we had a great time. We went up to the top of the Burj Khalifa. It's the tallest building in the world. It's VERY TALL! It looks like a building from a sci-fi movie! When we looked at the building from the ground I thought it would be scary to go up. But it wasn't. We bought our tickets and waited a bit and then we got into the lift.
It was a very fast lift and it took us up to the observation deck, which is near the top of the building. You can see the whole city of Dubai from the deck! It was awesome. I didn't want to go down again.
That's all for now. We're off to see a film this evening and I need to have a shower and get ready.
See you soon!
Mariam

2 Think of two places that you would like to visit. Do your own research on the internet and find something interesting about each place.

a Where is it?
b What can you see there?

3 Make a short presentation to your group or class.
Say what you think about the places you have researched.

a Why do people visit the place?
b Is the place well looked after?

Reading and speaking

1 Do you receive letters or emails from your friends or family? When do you get these? Why do people send you these letters or emails?

Letters

There are different types of letters. Letters are different because they are written for different **purposes** (why we write letters) and for different **audiences** (to whom we write letters).

2 Read the four texts on pages 12–13. Talk about the texts. Then answer the questions.

a What sort of texts are they?
b Who wrote each text and to whom?
c Why was each text written? What was the purpose of each text?
d What do you notice about the way the texts are organised?
e Which texts use more formal language? Find some examples of language that you think is formal.

Hi Lee,

It's my birthday and I'm having a party at my house on Saturday 8 June. I'd love you to come. It'll start at about two o'clock.

We're going to have fun. Hope you'll be able to make it?

C U soon.

Narinder

6 First Avenue
Pinewood
Inglestone Hills
IS4 7HL

2

Megaplay Games
Old Klang Road
Kuala Lumpur

Apartment B34
14 Jalan Senang
Kuala Lumpur

23rd September

Dear Sir/Madam

    I bought my son a Megaplay game console for his birthday. At first he enjoyed playing with it, but after a while it developed an annoying fault. Sometimes, halfway through the game, the screen goes blank. After that, he has to switch it off and start again. However, this doesn't stop it from happening again.

    In view of this, I would like a replacement console or my money back.

Yours faithfully,
Keith Nagaratnam

3

24 East Street
Grassy Park
Cape Town 7888

Dear Jo,

Just a quick note to say Happy Birthday. I hope you'll have a good party with your friends on Saturday.

Your mum tells me that you did well in your tests last week too. Well done!

Look forward to seeing you again at the end of the year.

Love,
Aunty Karen

4

Tolby Toys,
Victoria Industrial Estate,
Hong Kong

1 Southwood Heights,
Robertson Quay,
Singapore

31st March

Dear Sir/Madam,

    I saw your advertisement in the Singapore Echo newspaper, and would be grateful if you would send me your catalogue.

    I would also like to take advantage of your free gift offer for my early reply.

Yours faithfully,

Koh Ng

Word book

Add any unfamiliar words to your Word book.

Speaking and writing

1 PAIR WORK. Talk about the questions below. Then write the answers.

a What is the main purpose of Aunty Karen's letter?
b How does Aunty Karen know Jo did well in her test?
c What is the relationship between Narinder and Lee? How do you know this?
d How does Keith Nagaratnam's letter begin and end?
e Which other letter begins and ends in a similar way?
f Why do you think there are two addresses in Koh Ng's letter?
g Why do you think the endings in some of the letters are different from the endings in other letters?

2 PAIR WORK. Look at the different letters again. Make a chart to show the differences between the types of letters.

	From	Purpose	Greeting	Ending	Language
1					informal, friendly greeting and ending
2			Dear Sir/Madam		
3				Love	
4		To ask for a catalogue			

Remember!

The language used in letters can be different.

Some letters use formal language, for example: 'Dear Madam/Sir', 'Yours faithfully'.

Some letters use informal language, for example: 'Hi Kamel!', 'Love, Alina'.

Using pronouns

Copy the sentences below. Underline the pronouns.

a We are on holiday in Dubai. It is very hot here.
b I would love you to come.
c He has to switch it off and start again.
d We went up in a lift. It took us up to the observation deck.
e Look forward to seeing you again at the end of the year.

Pronouns

Pronouns are words that we use in place of nouns in sentences. Pronouns can be singular or plural. Here are some pronouns that we use often:

Singular	Plural
I you he she it	we you they
me him her	us them
mine yours his hers	our their
myself herself himself itself	themselves ourselves

Look at how we use pronouns in sentences.
'Maggie and her family went to the Burj Khalifa. They went up in the lift. It was very fast. Maggie enjoyed herself very much.'

Using verbs

1 Choose the correct verb for each sentence below. Write the correct sentences.

a Ali is from London. He (visits/visit) his family in Dubai every year.
b I (am going/are going) to visit the Taj Mahal next year.
c She (has/have) many cousins, aunts and uncles.
d We (is having/are having) a party next week.
e They went up in the lift. It (was/were) very fast.

Remember!

Pronouns must agree with the verbs. For example:

She **has** two sisters. (**She** is singular.)

We **have** two cars. (**We** is plural.)

2 **PAIR WORK.** Read the letters again. Find the same verbs in the box below in different forms.

> is   go   have   see   buy
>   will   do

Irregular verbs

Some verbs change when they describe actions in the past.

Example:
I **go** home every day after school.
Yesterday I **went** home.
Go and **went** are forms of the same verb.

Spelling and vocabulary

Words in dictionaries are arranged in alphabetical order. To find words quickly you need to know this order.

If words begin with the same letter, we look at the second letter in the word.

Write the words below in alphabetical order.

a screen   switch   start
b gift   game   great
c annoying   audience   again
d whole   want   would
e trip   ticket   test

camp camps
NOUN a place where you stay in a tent

centipede centipedes
NOUN a small animal with a long body and lots of small legs

charity charities
NOUN an organisation that helps people

cinema cinemas
NOUN a place where you can go to see a film (movie)

console consoles
NOUN a piece of equipment that you use to connect to a computer and play games

Using apostrophes

1. PAIR WORK. Find five sentences with apostrophes in the letters you have read on pages 12–13. Look at the informal letters.

2. Copy the sentences and circle the words with apostrophes.

3. Talk about what the complete words are. Say which letters are missing.

Apostrophes

When we speak, we often use informal language and we do not say all the letters in the words. To write these words we use an apostrophe (') to show that letters are missing. Here are some examples:

I'm = I am   can't = cannot
it's = it is   It'll = It will
you're = you are

Reading and speaking

GROUP WORK. Read the comic strip below aloud. Look carefully at the apostrophes.

I **can't** wait for the holidays.

We're going to India. **It'll** be such fun. **I've** never been there.

You're lucky. **I'd** love to go there too. **I'm** staying at home, but **we're** going to the game park.

Writing

1. Write a short letter to a friend. Invite your friend to come to your house or to join you on an outing.

2. Look at the letters from Aunty Karen and Keith Nagaratnam again.
   a. How many paragraphs are there in each letter?
   b. What information or idea is given in each paragraph?

Paragraphs

A paragraph is a section of a text. Each paragraph in a letter gives different information. We arrange text in paragraphs so that it is easy to read and understand.

3 Write a letter to someone in your family. Tell them about an outing you went on. Write three paragraphs. Use the plan below to help you.

[Write your address here]

[Write the date here]

Dear _____
[Paragraph 1: Say why you are writing the letter.]
_____
_____

[Paragraph 2: Describe what you did on the outing.]
_____
_____

[Paragraph 3: End with a greeting and mention when you will see the person again.]
_____
_____

Love
_____

Remember!

Look carefully at the way the letter is set out. Look at the address, the greeting and the ending and where they are on the page.

Spelling

Homophones

Homophones are words that sound the same but which have different meanings or spellings.

Read the sentences below aloud. What do you notice about the underlined words? Do you know what they mean? Use a dictionary if you are not sure.

a Do you <u>write</u> letters to your friends?
   What is the <u>right</u> way to end an email?

b There are <u>two</u> letters on the table for you.

Don't spend <u>too</u> much money when you go on holiday!

c She received <u>eight</u> emails yesterday.

I <u>ate</u> all my supper and I had desert afterwards.

d "Do you <u>know</u> where the Taj Mahal is?" asked Sami.

"<u>No</u>, I don't," replied Mateo.

e Why do we always start a letter with the word '<u>dear</u>'?

We saw a <u>deer</u> in the forest.

f I would like you to <u>meet</u> my sister, Tami.

Some people do not eat <u>meat</u>; they only eat vegetables.

Thinking time

- How do you know if a letter is formal or informal? What do you look for?
- What do apostrophes tell us about a text? How do you know when to use them or not?

3 Bugs

Reading and speaking

1 Complete the meaning below about the word 'bug'.

A bug is… It is also… and also…

Which meaning do you think 'bug' has in this poem?

2 What punctuation mark is used after the title? What do you think this means? Think about this as you read the poem.

3 Now read the poem aloud. Work out the meanings of words that are not familiar.

Let's talk about things that are useful
Let's talk about things you can't see.
It's time someone wrote a good poem
About very small creatures like ME.

Bugs!
We're everywhere.
We're in the water,
We're in the air.

Indoors, outdoors, underground,
Wherever you look that's where we're found.
We're on your hands and in your hair,
We're with you in the clothes you wear.

Bugs!
We can make your tummy funny,
Or a thousand noses runny.
Got a cut? Get a plaster.
Keep us out and you'll heal much faster.

Remember!

Words with similar letter patterns do not always sound the same, for example 'g<u>oo</u>d' and 'f<u>oo</u>d', or 'tr<u>ou</u>ble', 'f<u>ou</u>nd' and 'sh<u>ou</u>ld'.

We're the ones who make you ill,
Because of us you take that pill.
We're the ones who make you mad,
By turning good food into bad.

Bugs!
I agree, we don't sound good.
We cause more trouble than we should.
But ... let me tell you this about us,
People on Earth can't do without us.
In fact, you owe us such a lot!
If we weren't here to make things rot ...

... the pile of stuff you throw away
Would just get bigger every day.
Yes! We make things rot!
We make them *smell!*

Apple cores, potato skins,
All the scraps in all your bins –
We get to work and cause decay.
In time we rot it all away.
Rubbish mountains there would be,
If you didn't have my friends and me.

You need plants, and plants can't grow
Unless we're in the soil below.
We go to work on last year's leaves
Making food for next year's trees.
We get to work and cause decay,
In time we rot old leaves away.
Leaf mountains there would be,
If you didn't have my friends and me.

Bugs!
You can't see us,
But how you need us!
Because of all the work we do,
We make life possible for YOU.

So let's talk about things that are useful.
Let's talk about things you can't see.
It's time someone wrote a good poem
About very small creatures like ME.

By Sam McBratney

Reading and speaking

1 PAIR WORK. Talk about the questions below. Then answer the questions.

a Name two bad things that bugs do.
b Name two good things that bugs do.
c Where do you find bugs?
d Why does the earth need bugs?
e Why should you cover a cut with a plaster?
f Can bugs give you an upset tummy? How do you think this happens?

2 GROUP WORK. Read the poem aloud with expression.

Exclamation marks

Exclamation marks are used at the ends of sentences or after words to show strong feelings or surprise. When you read these words aloud, you should read them loudly.

How to read a poem aloud with expression

Make sure you understand what the poem means.

Look out for rhyming words at the end of each line and say the words clearly. Rhyming words help to give a poem rhythm.

Look at the punctuation marks:
- they will help you to know which words go together.
- they tell you when to pause.
- they tell you when to change your voice for exclamations and questions.

Listening and speaking

GROUP WORK. Talk about what you do with leaves and vegetable peels at home.

a Can you reuse these in any way?
b Do you have a compost heap?
c What is the best thing to do with leaves and vegetable peels? Why?

Reading and writing

1 Collect examples of nouns, verbs and adjectives from the poem *Bugs*. Write the words under the headings below.

| nouns | verbs | adjectives |

Remember!
Nouns name people, places and things. Verbs describe actions. Adjectives describe the nouns.

2 Write your own poem about bugs. Use some of the nouns, verbs and adjectives you wrote down. Use words that rhyme at the end of your sentences.

Start like this:

Bugs!
We're everywhere.
We're in _____
We're in _____
We're everywhere.

We can be bad.
We _____
We _____
We can be bad!

We can also be good.
We _____
We _____
We can also be good.

Word book
Add tricky words to your Word book.

Spelling: compound words

1 PAIR WORK. Look at the compound words in the box. Write the two shorter words that make up each compound word.

| underground   outdoors   everywhere |
| something   notebook   toothbrush |

Compound words
Compound words are made up of two shorter words. To spell and write a compound word, break the word into shorter words first and spell each shorter word.

2 Make six compound words with the shorter words in the box. Write the words.

| book   out   card   board   side   case |
| doors   bed   in   room   post   cup |

Reading and speaking

1 PAIR WORK. Before you read the next text, read all the headings and look at the illustration. Talk about the questions below.

a What is this text about?
b Is this text fact or fiction?

Non-fiction texts

Texts are pieces of writing. Some texts are fiction and others are non-fiction.

A **fiction** text is a text or a story that has been made up.

A **non-fiction** text has:
- **true** information or facts.
- **headings** that tell us what each section is about.
- **pictures** and **diagrams** that tell us more about the text.
- **captions** that tell us what pictures are about.

Germs

We use the word 'bug' to describe many different types of living things. For example, insects such as flies and ladybirds are often called bugs. And sometimes when we are ill, we say, "I've got a bug." In this case, the bugs are really germs that make us sick.

What are germs?
Germs are minute living organisms. They are so small that you need a microscope to see them. Germs live all over the world. They live inside our bodies, in our houses and outside in nature.

Different kinds of germs
There are different types of germs. The four main types are bacteria, viruses, fungi and protozoa.

Bacteria can live outside or inside our bodies. Some bacteria cause infections such as ear infections or tonsillitis. Other bacteria help us to digest our food or help plants to rot and form compost.

Viruses make us sick when they get inside our bodies. Viruses cause diseases like AIDS, flu and chickenpox.

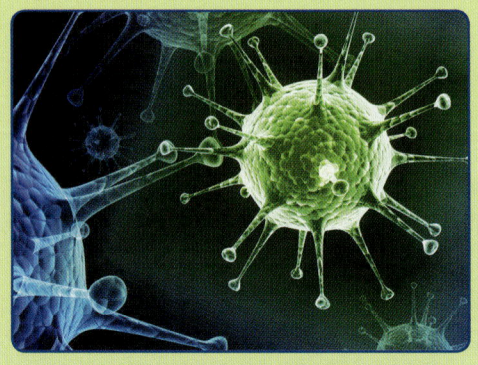

This is what a flu virus looks like if you look through a microscope.

24

Fungi live in dark, damp places. We can eat some fungi, such as mushrooms. Other fungi can cause skin rashes. For example, the rash that we sometimes get on our feet and between our toes is caused by fungi.

Protozoa live in wet conditions and spread diseases through water. They can give us tummy infections that lead to diarrhoea, vomiting and stomach ache.

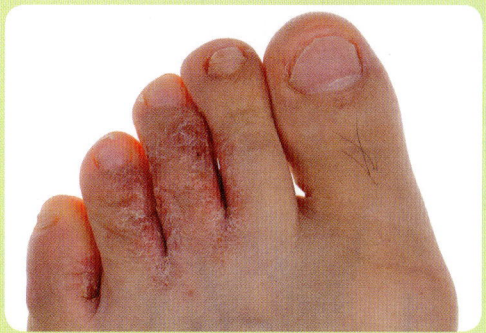

Athlete's foot is a skin condition caused by fungi.

Protect yourself from germs

Most germs are spread through the air when people sneeze or cough. Germs can also be spread through saliva and blood or by touching someone or something that has been infected with the germ. You can get a cold from shaking hands with someone who has a cold.

The best way to protect yourself from germs is by washing your hands. You should also cover your nose and mouth when you cough or sneeze so that you don't pass your germs on to other people who are near you.

2 **Scan the text again. Say if the statements below are true or false.**

a The bugs that make us sick are called 'germs'.
b Germs only live inside our bodies.
c Germs called 'bacteria' can cause infections.
d Protozoa live in dry places.

3 **Which of the statements below is an opinion, not a fact?**

a I hate coughing and sneezing.
b Germs can move through the air.
c Washing your hands helps to protect you from getting germs.

Remember!

Use a dictionary to check the meanings of words. Remember, words are in alphabetical order. If a word begins with *B* it will be near the front of the dictionary. If a word begins with *U* it will be near the end.

Reading and writing

Draw a chart like the one below. Complete your chart to make a summary of the information about germs in the text you have read. Make sure you use the correct words.

Types of germs	Where they live	What they do

Vocabulary: synonyms

Synonyms

We use adjectives like 'big' and 'small' all the time. But there are other more interesting words with the same meaning (synonyms) that we can use instead.

Look at these synonyms.
big: enormous, gigantic, tall, huge, great
small: tiny, minute, little, baby

Make the sentences below more interesting. Use synonyms for the underlined words. Write the new sentences. Underline the synonyms you used.

a   Germs are small living organisms.
b   There are lots of small insects in the garden.
c   He is a big boy.
d   She drew a big picture of a fly.
e   Help! There is a big rat in the kitchen!
f   The frog laid hundreds of small eggs in the water.

Reading

Find examples of statements, questions, exclamations and instructions in the texts you have read in this unit.

> **Remember!**
> Different types of sentences
> - <u>Statements</u> give us information. *Germs are living organisms.*
> - <u>Questions</u> ask for information. *What is a protozoa?*
> - <u>Exclamations</u> express feelings. *Bugs!*
> - <u>Instructions</u> give orders or directions. *Wash your hands with soap and water.*

Spelling: suffixes

PAIR WORK. Read the words in the box aloud.

| illness   infection   fiction   weakness |

a What do you notice? How do the words end?
b Write down four more words that you know that end in *–ion* or *–ness*.
c Check the spellings in a dictionary.

Listening and speaking

1. Listen to the instructions about how to wash your hands properly.
2. Tell a friend how to wash their hands properly.

Listening and writing

1. Listen to a text about how flies help to spread diseases.
2. Use the flowchart below to show what you heard. Write one sentence about each picture.

> **Thinking time**
> - How do you work out if a text is fact or fiction?

4 A good read

Listening and speaking

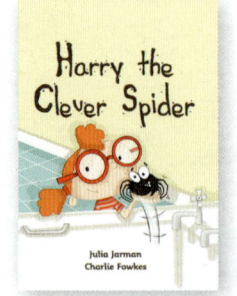
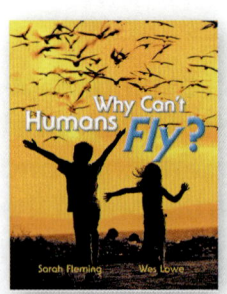

1. **GROUP WORK. Talk about the questions below.**

   a Do you enjoy fact or fiction books?
   b If you enjoy fiction, what type of stories do you enjoy?

   > adventure stories   historical stories   fantasy
   > love stories   folktales   myths and legends
   > comic stories   mystery   realistic stories

   c If you enjoy factual books, what subjects do you enjoy?

   > science   history
   > texts about real people   sports
   > geography   animals   plants

   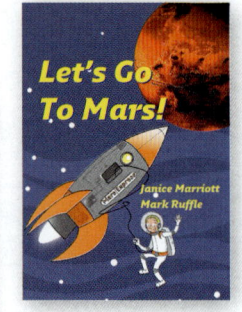

2. **PAIR WORK. Look at the names of the books in the list below. Talk about the books. What type of book do you think each one is?**

   > Achebe, Chinua: *How the Leopard Got His Claws*
   >
   > Dahl, Roald: *The Twits*
   >
   > Krishnaswami, Uma: *The Grand Plan to Fix Everything*
   >
   > Laird, Elizabeth: *Song of the Dolphin Boy*
   >
   > McNaughton, Colin: *Once Upon an Ordinary School Day*
   >
   > Willard, Hazel: *Odysseus and Polyphemus*

   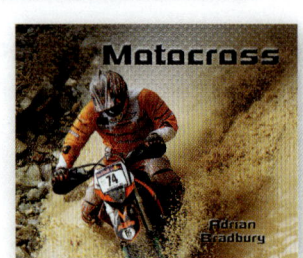

3 **Look at the list of books again. What do you notice?**

a Which name is first, the name of the writer or name of the book?
b Are the writers' first names or family names first?
c Are the names in alphabetical order?
d Why do we put lists in alphabetical order?
e Where else would you see lists in alphabetical order?

Reading

1 Read about the Dewey decimal system The Dewy decimal system is used to organise non-fiction books in a library.

The Dewey decimal system

The Dewey decimal system organises books according to numbers. There are ten main sections. For example, if you want to find a book about Africa, you would look on the shelf where there are books numbered 900–999.

Each main section is also divided into smaller sections. If you want to find books about famous painters, you would find them in the arts and leisure section (700–799), with numbers beginning with 750, which is the section about painters and painting.

000–099	General subjects
100–199	Philosophy
200–299	Religion
300–399	Social sciences
400–499	Languages
500–599	Science
600–699	Technology
700–799	Arts and leisure
800–899	Literature
900–999	History and geography

2. What numbers would you need to look for in the library if you wanted to find the information below? Write the answers.

a information about the history of India
b a diagram of the life cycle of a tomato plant
c pictures and lists of all the spaceships that have been launched
d a map of Africa
e a book about learning to speak French
f information about Christianity, Islam and Buddhism
g famous sprinters, like Usain Bolt

Reading and writing

1. Read the two book reviews below. What is the purpose of these texts? Why do you think they were written?

Song of the Dolphin Boy
by Elizabeth Laird

Set in small fishing village in Scotland, this story is about a boy called Finn. He is unhappy at home and he struggles to make good friends with the other children in the village. Then one day he dives into the sea and he finds that he enjoys swimming in the sea with the dolphins who live there. But his new friends, the dolphins, are in danger because of all the plastic people have thrown into the sea. Finn tries to help the dolphins, but this leads him to clash with people in the village.

This is another wonderful book by an award-winning writer. It has a strong message about the environment and about how we need to look after our planet. This is a fascinating adventure story – with a bit of fantasy too!

The Grand Plan to Fix Everything
by Uma Krishnaswami

Eleven years old and addicted to movies, Dini learns that her family is leaving the United States and moving to India. But they are not moving to Bombay, which is where many of the Bollywood movies starring her idol Dolly Singh are made. No! They are moving to town called Swapnagiri that is so small that Dini can't even find the place on a map. Dini is sad to leave her friend Maddie and convinced that life there will be very boring. But it isn't …

This book has all the fun and energy of a Bollywood movie as Dini makes new friends in Swapnagiri and keeps up her friendship with Maddie via her phone and the internet. It will make you laugh!

Book reviews

Book reviews:
- mention the characters, plot and setting of a book.
- give the reader an opinion about the book.

2   Write answers to the questions below.

a   Is *Song of the Dolphin Boy* fact or fiction?
b   Who wrote *The Grand Plan to Fix Everything*?
c   Who is the main character in *Song of the Dolphin Boy*?
d   Where is the story set? (Where does it happen?)
e   Books like these are arranged alphabetically in your library. Under which letters would you look for each book?
f   Do a search on the internet and write down the names of two more books by each writer. Find reviews of the books and find one book that you think you would like to read. Share this with a partner.

Reading and writing

1 Copy the chart. Complete your chart for the two books reviewed on pages 30 and 31.

Title	Song of the Dolphin Boy	
Writer		Uma Krishnaswami
Setting		
Characters		Dini, Maddie
Type of story	realistic	

2 Use the information in your chart to write a short note to a friend. Tell your friend about the book.

> **Remember!**
> If you are not sure what a word means, read the whole sentence again and see if you can work out the meaning. Look for clues in other sentences in the paragraph as well.

Vocabulary

1 PAIR WORK. Work out the meaning of the words below that were used in the book reviews. Then check in a dictionary to see if you are correct.

a clash   b environment   c idol   d addicted to

2 Look at the underlined words in the pairs of sentences below. Which words do you think are more interesting for the reader? Why do you think this?

Dini was <u>addicted</u> to movies.

This <u>good</u> story is about a boy called Finn.

This is a <u>fascinating</u> story.

Dini <u>liked</u> movies very much.

This <u>gripping</u> story is about a boy called Finn.

This is a <u>nice</u> story.

3 Copy the sentences below. Replace the underlined words with more interesting words.

a *The Rescue* is a <u>good</u> story about a boy who falls down a cliff.

b Have you read any <u>nice</u> books recently?

c My brother <u>likes</u> fantasy stories. I <u>don't like</u> them very much.

d The last Harry Potter book is <u>very big</u>.

Word book

Record any interesting words in your Word book and practise using them in your writing.

Using verbs

1 **PAIR WORK. Read the sentences below. Then answer the questions.**

- One day the boy into the sea.
- The dolphins in danger because of the plastic in the sea.
- Her grandmother ill.
- They to China next month.
- She that life in India would be very boring.
- I fantasy stories. They are so predictable and silly!

a What is missing in each sentence?
b Complete each sentence and read your sentences aloud to the rest of the class.
c Check that each sentence is grammatically correct.
d Which sentences were the most interesting? Why?

Remember!
All sentences have **verbs**. Without a verb, it is difficult to understand what a group of words mean.

Sentences with more than one clause

Some sentences have one verb with one subject. This means they have one clause. For example:

Uma Krishnaswami **is** an author.

Some sentences have more than one verb and subject, so they have more than one clause. The clauses are joined together with words such as 'and', 'so' or 'because'. Each clause has a verb. For example:

I **like** Uma Krishnaswami's books <u>because</u> they are always funny.

2 Read the paragraph below. Find the verbs and clauses in the sentences.

I have read *Fantastic Mr Fox* and I have seen the film *Charlie and the Chocolate Factory*. Roald Dahl wrote both of these stories. He became a famous writer because he wrote such wonderful stories. Children and adults all over the world have enjoyed his stories. Perhaps his stories are fascinating because he had such an interesting life. He was a boxing champion and he was also a fighter pilot.

Speaking, listening and reading

1 Look at the picture of the leopard. Read the caption. What do you know about leopards?

2 Talk about the answers to the questions below.

a What type of text is this – fiction or non-fiction?

b What do you think this text is about?

c What do you know about the writer?

3 Listen as your teacher reads the story aloud.

Leopards are big wild animals that live in Africa and Asia. They hunt for their prey at night.

This story is set in Kenya, in east Africa. A leopard has been prowling around in gardens and eating people's pets. Tom cannot find his pet cat, Tiger.

Tom Wilkinson turned off his light and pulled the curtains back from the main window.

He saw the little black cat at once. She was crouching in a pool of moonlight on the lawn, tense, as if ready to spring, looking intently ahead. Tom had watched her doing that hundreds of times before. She must have seen some little creature, a beetle or a toad and, cat-like, she was stalking it.

Without stopping to think, he ran downstairs again and dashed through the sitting room to the **verandah** doors. Dad had locked and bolted them before he'd gone up to bed, but the bolts were oiled and the locks new. It was easy to undo them. Tom opened the door and stepped out onto the verandah.

His heart was pumping painfully in his chest. He'd never been outside so late at night before.

He hesitated. The verandah, surrounded by man-made walls and roofed with man-sawn timbers, felt somehow safe, but the lawn was no-man's land. He'd be easy meat out there.

Why am I making such a big deal out of this? He thought. The leopard's probably miles away.

Tiger, intent on her prey, hadn't turned her head. She looked so innocent, so homely and tame, playing at being a hunter, that Tom couldn't imagine that any harm could come to her.

He took a deep breath, stepped off the verandah and ran towards the cat. Then he heard it, a deep, throaty cough, a warning, a threat, and he turned round and saw the leopard.

He was crouching in the shade of a tree and Tom could see only half of him, only the outline of one side of his head, one round ear, one spotted cheek and one stern, unwinking eye that seemed to frown at him from under a heavy brow.

From *Leopard Trail* by Elizabeth Laird

4 PAIR WORK. Reread the story.

5 Check the meanings of unfamiliar words in a dictionary.

6 Read the story again to yourself. Scan the text to find answers to the questions below.

a Who are the characters in this story?
b What is the setting (when and where does this happen)?
c How does Tom feel?
d Which of these characters is in the garden in this text?

> a leopard   Tom's pet cat, Tiger   Bella   Tom's dad

Listening and speaking

1 GROUP WORK. Write down words that describe the setting. Draw a picture of the setting from what you know.

2 What do we know about Tom's character in this story? Find sentences in the story that:

- tell us how Tom feels.
- describe what Tom does (his actions).

Share your ideas about what we know about Tom.

Using verbs

1 Read the sentences below from *Leopard Trail*. Look at the underlined verbs.

- Tom Wilkinson <u>turned</u> off his light and <u>pulled</u> the curtains back from the main window. He <u>saw</u> the little black cat at once.
- He <u>took</u> a deep breath, <u>stepped</u> off the verandah and <u>ran</u> towards the cat. Then he <u>heard</u> it, a deep, throaty cough, a warning, a threat, and he <u>turned</u> round and <u>saw</u> the leopard.

a What tense are the verbs?
b Why did the writer use this verb tense?
c Which verbs have irregular past tense forms?
d Match the present tense verbs in the box to the past tense forms in the sentences.

| hear | see | take | run |

2 GROUP WORK. Talk about what you think happens next in the story.

3 Now work alone. Write two paragraphs to describe what happened next. Use the past tense.

Remember!

We usually add –ed to make a past tense verb, but some verbs have irregular past tense forms. For example:
Tom <u>goes</u> outside. / Tom <u>went</u> outside yesterday.
He <u>hears</u> a noise. / He <u>heard</u> a noise.
If you are not sure of the form, look in a dictionary.

Spelling

PAIR WORK. Write a list of words with prefixes and suffixes in the story *Leopard Trail*.

Prefixes and suffixes

We add a prefix at the beginning of a word. Prefixes include *re–, in–, un–*.

We add a suffix at the end of a word. Suffixes include *–ed, –ing, –less, –ious, –ment*.

Word book

Add any tricky words with prefixes or suffixes to your Word book.

Reading and writing

1 Talk about and share information about your favourite writers as a class. Here are some things you could do:

- bring samples of the books to class to share and show others.
- read a text or a chapter from a favourite book to the class.
- let someone make a list of the names of the writers on a poster for reference.

2 Work alone. Go to the library and find two or three books by one writer. The books should each be 48–64 pages long and have several chapters.

3 Write a book review about one of the books you have read. Use the book review sheet that your teacher will give you.

4 Think about other books you have read by the same writer. How are the books similar or different? Read the questions below. Write notes to answer each question.

   a Are the characters in all the books the same?
   b Are the books fiction or non-fiction?
   c Did you like all of the books or did you like one book more than you liked the others?
   d Why did you enjoy the books? For example, were they funny, scary or interesting?

Speaking and listening

Give a short presentation to the class about the writer you have chosen. At the end of the presentations, give each other feedback. What went well? What could be improved and how?

- Read your review to the class. Make your review sound as interesting as possible.
- Ask the class a few questions, such as: Have you read this book? Do you think you would enjoy this book? Talk about your views and ideas.
- Tell the class about some of the other books that the writer has written. Use your notes about the books.
- Say which book or books you enjoyed the most and explain why.

Reading and writing

PAIR WORK. Look at the reviews you have written. Can you improve them by changing the order of the words in the first sentence you wrote? Talk about this. Then revise the first sentence in each review.

Improving your book reviews

Look at this sentence from one of the book reviews you have read. Notice how it begins. This grabs the attention of the reader.

Set in a small fishing village in Scotland, this story is about a boy called Finn.

Writing

1. Write a letter to your favourite writer. Invite the writer to visit your school. Plan the paragraphs you will write in the letter.
2. Read your letter carefully. Check your spelling and punctuation.

Remember!

Think carefully about the way a formal letter should be set out, and where you will put the address, the greeting and the ending.

Spelling

1. Read the words in the box aloud. Which *c* sounds are different?

> creature   crouch   kick
> concentrate   ancient

2. Rewrite the sentences below. Correct the spelling of the underlined words.

   a. Tom <u>looced</u> <u>bak</u> and saw the leopard <u>loocing</u> at him.
   b. My friends <u>licke</u> to <u>cik</u> a ball around the garden.
   c. The big <u>jinger</u> <u>kat</u> jumped up and over the wall.

The letters **c** and **k** are consonants. We often use them together at the ends of words as well –**ck**. The consonants can have the same sound, but we use them to spell different words. You need to remember how to spell these words. Make notes in your Word book. For example:

cat **k**itten lo**ck** (same sound)
centre **c**entimetre (different sound)

g and **j** are consonants that can sound different or they can sound the same. For example:

jump **g**inger (same sound)
garden **j**ar (different sound)

Reading

1 **Look at the text below. Answer the questions. Then read the text.**

  a Who wrote this story? What else have you read by this writer?
  b What do you think the underlined words in these sentences mean? Work out the meaning as you read the story if you are not sure.
  - Once there was a <u>shepherd</u> boy.
  - You have five sheep in your <u>fold</u>.
  - What is 4 <u>minus</u> 2?
  c Where is Ethiopia?

2 **Read the story silently until you understand what it is about.**

3 **Read the story aloud. Notice the direct speech in the story. Change your voice as you read what the different characters say.**

This is a story from Ethiopia.

Once there was a shepherd boy who started going to school. He found his lessons very difficult, and the hardest one of all was Maths.

"Take 3 from 5," the teacher said. "What's the answer?"

The boy shook his head.

"What's 4 minus 2?" asked the teacher. "You must be able to do that one."

But the boy couldn't.

"Well," the teacher said. "Here is an example you ought to understand. Say you have five sheep in your fold and one of them runs out through a hole in the fence. How many will you have left?"

"That's easy," the shepherd boy answers. "I won't have any left."

"How can you be so stupid?" asked the teacher.

"I'm not stupid!" said the boy. "I don't know much about Maths, but I know all about sheep. If one goes through a hole in the fence, all the others will follow!"

From *The Shepherd Boy at School* by Elizabeth Laird

Improve your reading aloud skills

Underline the words that you think are important so that you can give them emphasis.

Put a star (*) where you think you should pause. For example:

"What's 4 minus 2?" asked the teacher*.
"You must be able to do that one."

But the boy couldn't.

Thinking time

- What did you enjoy about sharing your favourite book?
- How did you decide whether you liked a book or not?

5 Amazing journeys

Reading and speaking

1 **Look at the contents and index pages of the book below. Then answer the questions.**

a How many sections or chapters are there in this book? (Do not count the glossary and index.)

b On which page would you find out about migration?

c What do you expect to find in the glossary?

d Antarctica is in the contents and in the index. On which pages would you look to find out about Antarctica?

e Which page do you think could tell you about how humpback whales grow?

2 **PAIR WORK. Take turns to ask and answer questions about the contents and index pages.**

> **Finding information in a non-fiction book**
>
> The **contents** page is at the beginning of a book. The contents page tells us about the main sections or chapters into which the book is divided. It also gives page numbers.
>
> The **index** is at the back of the book. The index tells you where you can find information about particular ideas or subjects.

The Journey of Humpback Whales

Contents

Humpback whales	2
The journey of humpback whales	8
Migration: a huge journey	14
Life in Antarctica	18
Glossary	20
Index	21
The life cycle of humpback whales	22

Written and photographed by Andy Belcher

Collins

Index

Antarctica	8, 9, 16, 18, 19
barnacles	6
blowholes	2
boats	16, 17
breaching	6, 7
calves	9, 11, 12, 14, 16, 18
diving	4, 5
feeding	18, 19
krill	18
mating	8, 9
migrating	8, 9
sea lice	6
Tonga	9, 14

Vocabulary

1. Before you read the text, scan it quickly and write any words that look unfamiliar.

2. Look at the purple words in the text on pages 41 and 42. Try to work out the meanings of these words as you read. Check the meanings in the glossary if you are not sure.

Reading non-fiction

Read the headings and look carefully at the pictures before you read the text.

Remember!

If you are not sure what a word means, think of similar words that you know.

Example: 'migrate'

Perhaps you know the word 'migrant', which means a person who travels to other countries to look for work. So the verb 'migrate' has something to do with travelling to other places.

The Journey of Humpback Whales

Humpback whales

Humpback whales are **mammals**, not fish. This means they can't breathe underwater. Humpbacks have two big nostrils – blow holes – on the top of their heads, and must come to the surface of the water to breathe.

The journey of humpback whales

Humpbacks have swum in our oceans for up to ten million years. They live for about 50 years and during their lifetime they may swim 800 000 kilometres. This is because every two years at the end of winter the humpbacks **migrate** to have their babies.

At the age of five the female whales will mate. When they are pregnant they swim 5600 kilometres from Antarctica to Tonga. The baby whales, called calves, live inside their mothers for 11 months. They have a better chance of **survival** if they're born in the warmer water near Tonga.

Did you know?
Whales sleep with one half of their brain while using the other half to keep swimming.

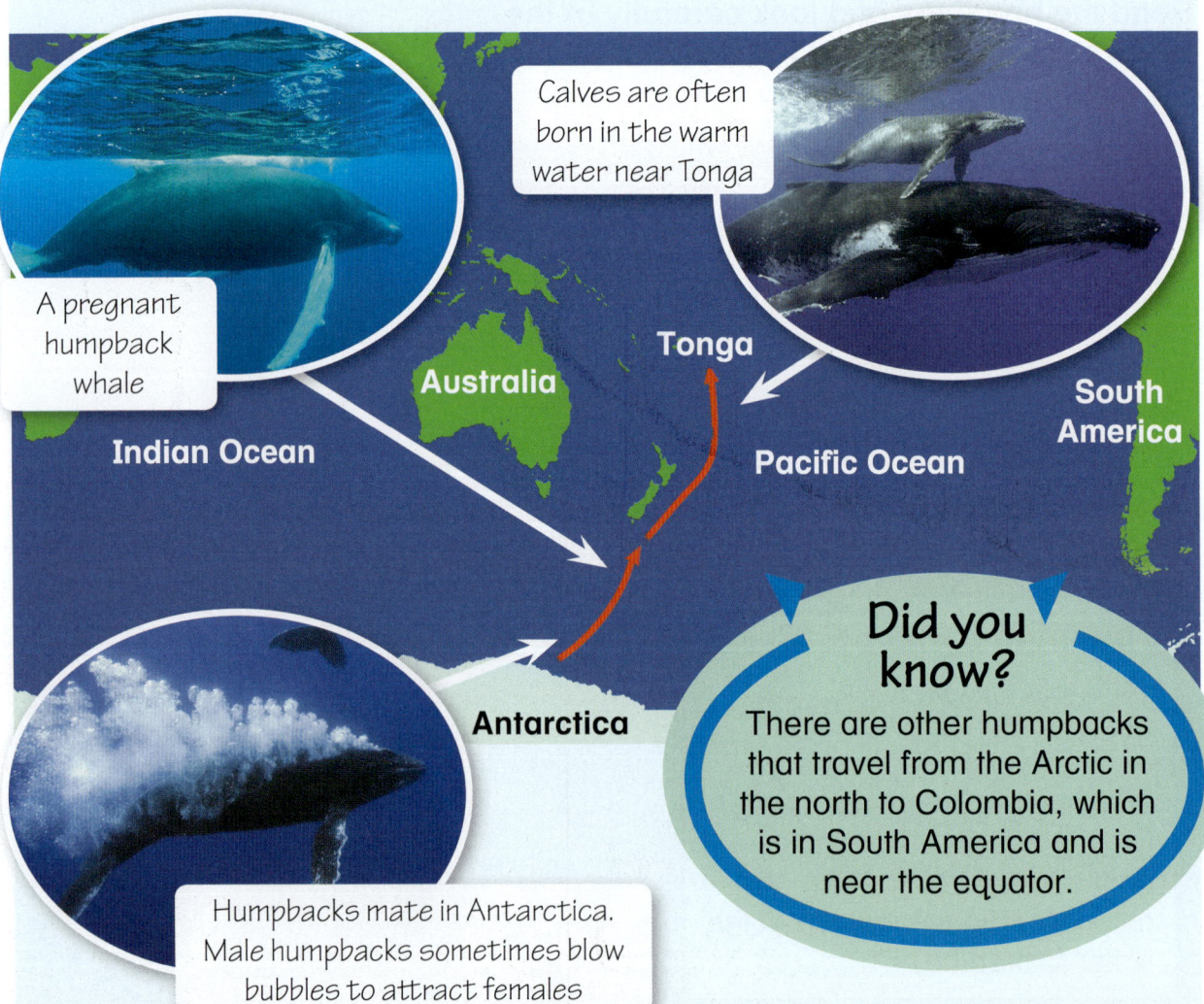

A pregnant humpback whale

Calves are often born in the warm water near Tonga

Indian Ocean

Australia

Tonga

Pacific Ocean

South America

Antarctica

Humpbacks mate in Antarctica. Male humpbacks sometimes blow bubbles to attract females

Did you know?
There are other humpbacks that travel from the Arctic in the north to Colombia, which is in South America and is near the equator.

Migration: a huge journey

But there's no food for the mothers in the waters around Tonga. They survive by living off the layer of fat, or blubber, under their skin. After two months in Tonga mothers and calves must swim back to Antarctica, where there is food. The journey south takes two to three months and the mothers swim with their calves day and night.

Although humpbacks are very big, they still face dangers like strong currents, storms, getting caught in fishing nets or being hit by boats. A few calves may die from shark attacks but most arrive safely in Antarctica.

Life in Antarctica

The humpback's main food is krill, a tiny pink shrimp-like animal. Antarctica has roughly 300 million tonnes of krill so the mothers and their calves stay and feast for two years until the mothers are pregnant again and they swim the 5600 kilometres back north.

Glossary

mammals: animals that breathe air, have warm blood and give birth to babies which the females feed with milk

migrate: travel long distances at the same time each year, to feed, mate or give birth

survival: staying alive

Reading and writing

Scan the text again to find the answers to the questions below. Write your answers.

a Are humpback whales mammals or fish?
b How many kilometres does a humpback swim during its life time?
c How far is it from Antarctica to Tonga?
d How long does it take the whales to swim from Tonga back to Antarctica?
e Why do the whales swim to Tonga?
f What does a humpback eat?
g Name two dangers that the whales have to face in the water.

Spelling

Remember!
Suffixes are letters that we add to the ends of words. We can use suffixes to make new adjectives, verbs, nouns and adverbs.

1 Copy the words below. Circle the suffix in each word. Think of three other words that end in the same suffix. You could make a chart like the one below.

Word	Suffix	Other words with same suffix
survival	–al	arrival, musical, cultural, official
warmer		
roughly		

Singular and plural nouns

With most nouns we can form a plural by adding –s or –es. But some nouns have irregular plural forms. Look at these examples:

calf calves   child children   baby babies
man men   loaf loaves   knife knives

2 GROUP WORK. Have a quiz. Choose the correct plural form for each of the words below. Use a dictionary to check your answer. See which group can answer all the questions correctly first.

- a woman: wemen/women
- b country: countres/countries
- c half: halves/halfs
- d knife: knifes/knives
- e child: childes/children
- f goose: gooses/geese
- g loaf: loafers/loaves
- h mouse: mouses/mice
- i tooth: tooths/teeth
- j ox: oxes/oxen

Word book

Write the correct plural words in your Word book.

Listening and speaking

PAIR WORK. Listen to the text your teacher will read to you. Act out what the cuckoos do.

eurasian cuckoo

Writing a non-fiction text

Many animals migrate. Some animals have made amazing journeys because they have wanted to reach a certain place. Find out about one of the journeys below. Then plan and write a description of it.

STEP 1 Use the internet or the library to find out about some of these journeys.

Remember!
If you are looking for information in the library, look for books with Dewey decimal numbers between 590–599 (Science, animals).

Some amazing journeys

- the journeys made by huge herds of wildebeest every year when the Serengeti area where they live becomes too dry
- the migrations of salmon fish from the ocean to fresh water to lay their eggs
- the migrations of monarch butterflies
- the journey of Huberta the hippo in South Africa
- the journey of Lin Wang, the old elephant, who travelled miles across Burma and China

STEP 2 Decide which journey you want to write about.

STEP 3 **Plan your text.**
- How many sections or paragraphs will you have?
- Will you use headings? What will the headings be?
- Will you add pictures? Remember to write captions to go with the pictures.
- How will you present the text? On a printed sheet? On screen?

STEP 4 **Draft your text.**

STEP 5 **Now check your text and then improve it.**
- Have you used the correct vocabulary and spelt the names of places correctly?
- Have you used capital letters and full stops?
- Type your text on a computer and use the spellcheck to check your spelling.
- Use letters in different sizes or colours to make the text more interesting.

STEP 6 **Reflection.**
- What did you enjoy about writing this description?
- How did you decide about how to present the description?

Speaking to an audience

Present your description of an amazing journey. Explain why you were interested in the story. Then read your story aloud to other learners in your school.

Remember!
- Adapt your tone of voice. You are not chatting to your friends!
- Speak loudly and clearly but don't shout.
- Don't speak too fast.
- Emphasise some words to make the text more interesting.
- Try to sound enthusiastic and interested!
- Smile and look at the audience as you read.

Reading and speaking

1 GROUP WORK. Talk about the answers to the questions below. Use a dictionary if you are not sure.

a An explorer is …
- a person who travels to new places.
- a person who goes to places on holiday.

b Antarctica is near the …
- South Pole.
- North Pole.

c A base camp is …
- a place which is the centre of an operation.
- a very small campsite with basic equipment.

d A sledge is …
- a plough which removes snow.
- a vehicle pulled by animals which transports people and goods across snow or ice.

2 PAIR WORK. Read the text below. What type of text is it? What is the purpose of the text?

Captain Scott: Journey to the South Pole

Adrian Bradbury

Captain Robert Falcon Scott was a British naval officer and explorer. In June 1910, Scott and a team of men left Britain for Antarctica. At that time, no one had ever reached the South Pole in Antarctica and Scott wanted to be the first.

Scott's boat reached the Antarctic in January 1911. It had to get there in the Antarctic summer, so the ship could break through

the ice to get to land. After setting up a base camp, the men had to wait through the long, dark Antarctic winter. Only in the following summer would it be warm and light enough to set out for the South Pole.

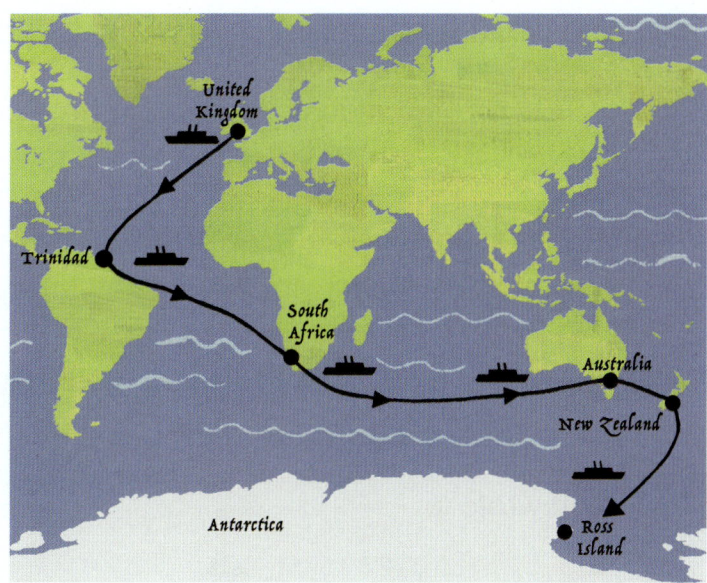

On 2 November 1911, Scott and nine other men set out with ponies. The final four men followed later with dogs. The South Pole was nearly 1500 kilometres away.

The motor sledges broke down after 80 kilometres. The ponies were not used to the freezing weather and, one by one, they died.

The dogs were sent back to the base camp because there was no food left to feed them. Now the men had to pull the sledges themselves. The men needed extra food, but Scott had not made any plans for this. They grew weaker and began to slow down.

Scott planned that most of the men would turn back at stages along the way. Only five men made the last step of the journey to the South Pole. The men reached the South Pole on 17 January 1912, 76 days after they had set out.

But they were not the first to get there. Another explorer, Norwegian Roald Amundsen had beaten them. Bitterly disappointed and very tired, the men were faced with the same journey they had just completed to get back to base.

But Scott and his men were very tired and the weather got worse and worse. The temperature dropped to minus 40 degrees Celsius. On 29 March 1912 Scott wrote in his diary:

"The end cannot be far. It seems a pity but I do not think I can write more."

Without food or fuel to heat water, they could not survive. Eight months later, their tent was found, along with their bodies.

3 **PAIR WORK. Make a list of six questions to use in a class quiz. Write the questions and answers.**

Example:
What nationality was Captain Scott? (Answer: British)

Remember!

Use a question mark (?) at the ends of your questions.

4 **GROUP WORK. Ask your questions. Take turns and see which pair in each group can answer the most questions correctly. Your teacher will help you work out a way to score.**

Spelling

Write the paragraph below in the past tense. Change the verbs in brackets in each sentence.

Captain Scott (want) to be the first man to reach the South Pole. He and his team had a long and difficult journey. They (need) more food and some men even (pull) the sledges. But when Scott (arrive) at the South Pole, Amundsen had beaten them to it! Scott and Amundsen both (reach) the South Pole in 1912.

> **Remember!**
> Most verbs in the past tense end in –ed.
>
> Example:
> play → played
> survive → survived.

Linking words

PAIR WORK. Read the texts below. Find the linking words in each paragraph.

a Whale mothers live off the fat in their skin while their calves are small. After two months in Tonga, mothers and calves must swim back to Antarctica.

b Scott's boat reached Antarctica in the summer of January 1911. Only in the following summer would it be warm and light enough to set out for the South Pole.

c Without food or fuel to heat water they could not survive. Eight months later, their tent was found, along with their bodies.

> **Remember!**
> Words at the beginning of a sentence can help to link the sentences to events that happened before. In the paragraph below, the words At that time link sentences.
>
> In June 1910, Scott and a team of men left Britain for Antarctica. At that time, no one had ever reached the South Pole in Antarctica and Scott wanted to be the first.

Writing

Imagine you are Roald Amundsen. Write a description of how you felt and what you saw on the day you reached the South Pole. Remember to link the ideas in your description.

Today we finally reached the South Pole! We travelled for 33 days and we all feel …

> **Thinking time**
> Which words did you use to link your ideas about Roald Amundsen? Think about two ways these kind of words improve a piece of writing.

6 Myths and legends

Reading and speaking

Legend (noun) A legend is a story about a person and his or her actions. A legend is usually based on some true facts but many are not completely true. Many legends tell of things that the person didn't actually do, or they exaggerate to make the story more interesting or to teach a lesson.

Myth (noun) A myth is a made-up story used to explain how parts of the natural world work or to teach a lesson in how to behave. They are usually set a very long time ago, before people wrote things down and recorded history. Myths often involve things that we know are not possible, for example: flying dragons, animals that can talk or human beings who make thunder and lightning.

1. **Read the definitions in the box. Answer the questions below.**

   a What is the main difference between a myth and a legend?

   b Dragons are mythical creatures. Can you think of any other mythical creatures?

   c Do you know any legends? Tell the class about them.

2. **PAIR WORK. Read the story of *Tiddalik the Frog*. Answer the questions below.**

   a Is this a myth or a legend? How do you know? What is the theme?

   b Who are the characters in the story?

   c Where is the story set?

   d Are there any words you don't know? Try to work out what they mean.

Word book

Write the words 'myth' and 'legend' in your Word book.

TIDDALIK THE FROG

(An Aboriginal Dreamtime story from Australia)
Retold by Karen Morrison

Tiddalik was the largest frog in the whole of the Australian outback. He was large and green and very, very thirsty.

One afternoon, after a long, dry sleep, Tiddalik woke up with an enormous thirst.

"I'm so thirsty I could lap up this water hole," he complained. And that is what he did. He drank and drank till the water hole was dry. After that Tiddalik was much fatter than before, but he was still thirsty. "But I see a nice full stream," he muttered. So, he hopped over to the nice full stream and he drank it dry.

Next was the lake. When the lake was dry, Tiddalik was still thirsty but he'd swelled up so much that he could hardly move.

"But I'm still thirsty," he thought. So he moved around, slowly, drinking and drinking till there was no fresh water left anywhere in the land.

By night time, Tiddalik was no longer thirsty, but he was so swollen with water that he couldn't move. He decided to take a nap, right where he was, in the shade of a large gum tree.

The next day, the sun rose on a dry land. There was no water anywhere. The trees and grasses withered and flopped over. The insects, birds and other animals searched for water, but there was none to be had.

The animals knew they had to do something or they'd all soon die of thirst. But they didn't know what they could do to get the water back from the greedy frog who was sleeping peacefully under his tree.

Eventually a wombat had an idea. "I think we should make Tiddalik laugh," he explained. "That way he'll open his wide mouth and the water will flow out and we'll all be able to have some water." The animals all agreed that this was a good plan.

The animals crowded round Tiddalik. Kangaroo nudged him with her foot to wake him up. Kookaburra told his best jokes in his loudest voice, and he laughed and laughed at his own jokes till he fell over. Tiddalik just blinked.

The lizards did a clumsy dance, backwards and forwards. Tiddalik just blinked again. Kangaroo did some high hops, backwards jumps and boxing moves. Tiddalik didn't even bother to blink.

The emus fluffed their feathers and pecked madly at each other. The other animals fell about laughing. Tiddalik looked a little amused, but he didn't even smile.

"What shall we do?" the animals cried. They were hot, and tired, and thirsty and Tiddalik hadn't spilled a drop of water.

Later in the afternoon, an eel wiggled out from under his sleeping rock. "Where is the water? It's all gone," he moaned. Eel crawled towards the animals gathered around Tiddalik. But the sand was hot and he couldn't crawl over it, so he tried to stand up on the end of this tail.

Eel struggled to balance on the end of his tail. He wobbled one way and another, and he bent himself into all sorts of shapes trying to avoid the hot ground.

Tiddalik stared at the eel. Eel hopped and bopped and twisted and jived trying to keep his balance.

As Tiddalik watched the unhappy eel, he started to smile. His smile got bigger and bigger till he started to giggle.

Finally he laughed out loud and his mouth opened wide. As Tiddalik laughed and laughed, the water gushed out of his mouth, filling the streams, the lakes and the water holes all over the land.

"Thank you, Eel!", the animals shouted. "It was you who made Tiddalik laugh." But Eel didn't even hear them, he was so happy to be swimming around in lovely cool, muddy water again.

Reading and speaking

1 PAIR WORK. Answer the questions below.

a In which country is this story set?
b Find three words in the story that describe the setting (Where is it? What is it like? What can you see there?)
c What did Tiddalik do?
d How did Tiddalik's actions affect the plants and animals in the environment?
e What did the wombat suggest they do to solve the problem?
f How did the kookaburra try to make Tiddalik laugh?
g Which animal made Tiddalik laugh? How?

2 GROUP WORK. Talk about the questions below.

a Why do you think the Aboriginal people told this story?
b How is this different from an adventure story?
c What sort of character is Tiddalik?
d Tiddalik drinks all the water. How does this affect the environment?
e What does this myth teach us about sharing and fairness?
f Why do you think the animals tried to make the frog laugh rather than hurting him to spill the water?

Working in groups

- Choose a group leader and ask someone to take notes if necessary.
- Respond politely and say what you think.
- Add new ideas to the group talk if you can.
- Listen to the ideas of others.
- Take turns to speak.

Reading and speaking

Find the dialogue in the story. Read the words aloud with expression. Imagine you are the character who speaks the words.

Dialogue

Writers put **dialogue** in stories to make the stories more real. The dialogue is always in speech marks (inverted commas) (" ") so that the readers know that these are the words the character said.

Vocabulary

1. In the story about Tiddalik, the writer uses dialogue but she does not always use the words 'said' or 'asked' after the dialogue. Find seven words the writer uses instead of 'said'.

2. Copy the dialogues below. Copy the punctuation carefully. Change the word 'said' to a more interesting word.

   a "I am so thirsty!" said Tiddalik.
   b "Tiddalik is very greedy," said the wombat.
   c "Wake up, Tiddalik!" said the kangaroo.
   d "I need water to swim in," said the eel.
   e "That's a funny story!" said the kookaburra.
   f "You emus look so funny," said the other animals.

Listening and speaking

1 You are going to listen to a myth called *Tiddalik the Flood Maker*.

   a What do you predict this myth will be about? How do you think it will end?

   b What do you already know about a character called Tiddalik?

2 Look at the pictures of the animals below. Are any of these characters in the story that you already know?

Koala

Echidna

Kookaburra

Eel

3 Listen to the myth. Then talk about the answers to the questions below.

   a Which characters from the myth that you read are *not* in this version of the myth?

   b Is the plot more or less the same, or is it different?

4 GROUP WORK. Act out the version of the myth you enjoyed most. Use lots of actions and movement to create the characters in the myth.

Remember!

The way a character moves tells us a lot about their character. Tiddalik is big and lazy, so he moves slowly and with heavy footsteps. Lizards have short legs so when they dance they look clumsy.

> **Sentences with more than one clause**

> ### Conditionals
>
> Some sentences have more than one clause. These sentences have more than one verb. The clauses are joined by connecting words such as 'and'. For example:
>
> Tiddalik *was* a large green frog **and** he *was* very thirsty.
>
> Some clauses are joined with the word 'if'. 'If' links the events in the two clauses. The event in one clause will be the result of the event in the other clause. We call these conditional clauses. For example:
>
> '**If** I *roll* down the bank, Tiddalik *will laugh*,' thought Echidna.

1 Think about the story of Tiddalik. Copy and complete the sentences below. Use clauses from the box.

> Tiddalik will laugh   it will quench my thirst
> If we don't have water to drink   he will have to open his mouth

a "If I drink that water in the billabong, _____," thought Tiddalik.

b The animals thought, "If we can make Tiddalik laugh, _____."

c Kookaburra thought, "If I tell a funny story, _____."

d The animals thought, "_____, we will all die."

2 Read the complete sentences aloud.

Reading

1 Read the two famous legends on pages 59 and 60 quietly on your own. Talk about the two legends and compare them. Then answer the questions.

    a Who are the main characters in each legend?
    b Where and when is each legend set?
    c What is special about the things that each character does? What is their motive or reason for doing this?
    d Are any parts of these legends based on real history? Which parts of these stories may be true?

THE LEGEND OF ODYSSEUS

Odysseus (say: O–di-si -us) was a legendary king in ancient Greece. He ruled an island kingdom called Ithaca. It is said that he was a wise and clever man.

Odysseus lived at a time, more than 3000 years ago, when there was a war between the Greeks and the Trojans. The Trojans lived in the part of the land that is now Turkey. The leaders of the different Greek kingdoms persuaded Odysseus to lead the Greek armies. The war lasted ten years and Odysseus helped the Greeks to win the war.

Then Odysseus and his army started a long journey home by sea. The journey was full of adventures. There were terrible storms that blew the ships to faraway places. The men had to fight against many strange creatures. One creature was a one-eyed giant called the Cyclops. He caught some of the soldiers and Odysseus had to come up with a clever plan to escape. They also had to get past beautiful bird-like creatures called the Sirens. The Sirens sang songs that caused sailors on boats to come too close to the rocks on their island. Their ships broke on the rocks and the ships sank.

Finally, after ten years, Odysseus and his army arrived home on the island of Ithaca.

The Legend of the Queen of Sheba

Makeda, Bilgis, Belkis, Nkuale, Ayab ile Seba – these are all names by which the legendary Queen of Sheba was known in different cultures. She was born in the 10th century BCE and ruled over an ancient kingdom called Sheba. We are not sure where the Queen of Sheba lived, but we think it was in the area where Yemen and Ethiopia are today.

According to the legend, the queen had heard about the wisdom of the King of Judea, King Solomon. She decided to visit him in Jerusalem. She made a famous journey to visit the king. She took a whole caravan of camels as well as gifts of spices and gold for the king.

The queen was said to be very beautiful.

2 Do some research to find out the answers to the questions below.

    a Who wrote a famous poem about Odysseus?
    b What did the ancient Romans call Odysseus?
    c What were the names of the wife and son of Odysseus?
    d How did Odysseus and his men get away from the Cyclops?
    e Where is the island of Ithaca in modern Greece? Find it on a map.

Now use the internet to find out the answers.

Listening and speaking

Your teacher will read two different versions of the story of what happened when Odysseus and his men met a Cyclops. Compare the two versions.

Writing

Use the internet to find out about a legend from your own country. Your teacher will give you some suggestions. Write a paragraph to explain the legend.

Using verds

Write the sentences below in the past tense. Change the verbs in brackets in each sentence.

a Odysseus (become) a Greek hero and legend.
b Tiddalik (drink) all the water in the land.
c The bird (tell) us some funny jokes.
d After hearing that story, I (feel) quite sad.
e Yesterday the sun (shine) in the morning but then it (rain) in the afternoon.
f The frog (think) that he was still thirsty, so he (go) to the lake and drank all the water in the lake.

Remember!

Many verbs have irregular past tense forms. You need to learn to recognise and spell these words.

Examples:
blow → blew
feel → felt
become → became
shine → shone

Reading

 Read the myth below by yourself.

The Wind and the Sun

This story is one of Aesop's fables and it is also told by the Akan people of Ghana.

One day long ago the wind and the sun had an argument.

"I am the strongest and most important force in the weather," said the wind, who was quite a boastful character.

"I disagree," said the sun. "Each of us has an important job to do. We are equal."

But the wind was stubborn. "I agree that all weather is important and strong," exclaimed the wind, "but I am the strongest of all."

So they decided to have a competition to prove who was stronger. "You see that man walking down the road? Which one of us can get the man to take his jacket off? That person will be the strongest weather," declared wind.

The wind began. He blew strong gusts of air at the man. The man could hardly walk because the wind was so strong. But he didn't take his jacket off – in fact he clutched it more tightly around his body. The wind blew and blew and blew – until he was exhausted!

Then it was the sun's turn. The sun gently shone down in the man. He soon took off his jacket, then his shoes and then his socks. Then he went to find a shady tree.

The wind was very angry that he had lost the competition, but the sun said, "Remember, we are all strong and we each have a job to do. I need to warm up the earth so that people are not cold and the crops can grow. You need to blow the clouds across the sky when there is too much rain and create a breeze when it gets very hot. We are a team and we should work together!"

2 Write your answers to the questions below.

a Who are the main characters in this story?
b What was the argument about?
c What did the characters decide to do?
d Who won the competition?
e Who was angry about the result of the competition?
f What lesson can we learn from this story? Choose the best answer.
- The one who shouts the loudest always wins.
- Gentle persuasion is stronger than force.

Writing

Write your own myth in the same style as the myth you have just read.

- Describe the setting for the myth.
- Include some dialogue in your myth. Use the present tense in the dialogue and speech marks.
- Use the past tense for the other sentences.
- Include sentences with more than one clause and use sentence openings to link ideas.
- Write your story in paragraphs.
- Remember that myths often teach lessons.

Description

The setting of a story is the place where the story occurs, but it is also the time when the story occurs. Use phrases to describe the setting of a myth, for example:

Once upon a time …
Long, long ago …
A long time ago …

Thinking time

- What did you enjoy about reading and listening to myths and legends?
- What did you do to make the myth that you wrote interesting?
- Why is it important to mix description with direct speech? Think about what a story would be like if it was all direct speech.

7 On stage

Listening and speaking

Your teacher will read you part of a story called *Tiger Dead! Tiger Dead!* The story features a character called Anansi, whom you may remember. In this chapter of the story, one of the characters plots to take over the forest so that he can have it all to himself.

1 Look at the list below of the characters in the story. Try to imagine how they would speak and move. Now listen to the story.

Tiger Mrs Tiger Anansi

Tortoise Rabbit Lizard Duck

2 Listen carefully to the order in which things happen in the story.

3 PAIR WORK. Retell the story to each other.

4 PAIR WORK. Talk about the characters in the story. Ask each other questions.

- Are they silly, proud, cunning, wise or greedy?
- Do they think before they act?
- Do the characters all tell the truth?
- How do you think the characters move and talk?

Reading instructions

Read the instructions below about how to make a mask as a prop to use in a play.

You will need
- a small, white paper plate or a piece of cardboard the size of your face
- a pair of scissors
- pencil and coloured crayons or pens
- a stick
- some tape to attach the stick to the mask

What you do
- Make sure the plate or cardboard is the right size. It should just cover your face.
- Draw and colour in a picture of your character on the plate.
- Cut out the eyes carefully.
- Attach the stick to the bottom of the plate, at the back.

Props
Props are anything that you use in a play to help the audience understand the play, for example: a mask, a costume or a piece of furniture.

Reading and speaking

GROUP WORK. Act out the part of *Tiger Dead! Tiger Dead!* that you listened to.

- Think about how the characters speak and what each character does.
- Use your face mask or name tags if you want to use props.

Remember!
Think about these questions when you talk about the **characters** in this story:
- What kind of animals are they?
- How do they talk?
- How do they move?

Reading a playscript

1 Before you read the play on pages 66–68, read the title and look at the list of characters. Read the names. Do you know the story?

Chicken Licken   Henny Penny   Cocky Locky   Foxy Loxy

Ducky Lucky   Drakey Lakey   Gander Lander   Goosey Loosey   Turkey Lurkey

2 Think about the setting of the play. The story is set in an oak forest. Oak trees have acorns, which are seeds.

   a Look at the picture below carefully. Describe what an acorn looks like.
   b The play has three scenes. Is the setting the same for each scene?

Playscripts

Plays are divided up into **acts** and **scenes**.

The **setting** describes where the events take place.

The **names of the characters** are written on the left, often in capital letters and followed by a colon (:). This makes it easy for the actors to find their lines.

The text in italic script gives the actors **instructions**.

3 Now read the scenes from the play aloud.

Chicken Licken
A traditional story

Characters

Henny Penny	Drakey Lakey	Turkey Lurkey
Cocky Locky	Goosey Loosey	Foxy Loxy
Ducky Lucky	Gander Lander	

Scene 1: *CHICKEN LICKEN is taking a walk in an old oak forest. A big green acorn falls on his head.*

CHICKEN LICKEN: Ouch! What was that? *(He looks up at the sky.)* Oh no! The sky's falling down! I must go and tell the king!

(He races off and bumps into HENNY PENNY.)

HENNY PENNY: You're in a hurry! Where are you going?

CHICKEN LICKEN: *(panting)* The sky's falling down and I must go and tell the king!

HENNY PENNY: The sky's falling down? Are you sure?

CHICKEN LICKEN: Yes, yes. I'm in a hurry.

HENNY PENNY: I'd better come with you.

(They race off together.)

Scene 2: *Further along the path in the forest.*

COCKY LOCKY: Hey! Watch where you are going! You nearly knocked me over!
CHICKEN LICKEN: Sorry … in a hurry … big trouble …
HENNY PENNY: Chicken Licken says the sky is falling down. We're off to tell the king!
COCKY LOCKY: We'll all die if that happens. I'm coming with you!

(The excited animals race off together.)

Scene 3: *Near some water in the forest. The three meet DUCKY LUCKY, GOOSEY LOOSEY, GANDER LANDER and DRAKEY LAKEY*

DUCKY LUCKY: *(slowly coming out of the water)* What's up?
GOOSEY LOOSEY: *(shaking herself off)* Why are you running?
GANDER LANDER: *(shaking his head)* What a noise!
DRAKEY LAKEY: *(looking surprised)* What's going on?
CHICKEN LICKEN: The sky … *(puffing and panting)*
COCKY LOCKY: *(also puffing and panting)* I bumped into Chicken Licken and Henny Penny – or rather – they bumped into me! Anyway, Henny Penny says that Chicken Licken says that the sky is falling down! We are going to tell the king.
DRAKEY LAKEY: So let me get this straight … Henny Penny saw Cocky Locky and the King, who says that the sky …
GANDER LANDER: NO! NO! NO! They're going to tell the king that the sky is falling down.
GOOSEY LOOSEY: Uh?? I'm confused …

Scene 4: Coming out of the forest, the seven meet TURKEY LURKEY and FOXY LOXY

TURKEY LURKEY:	(fluffing up his feathers and looking important) I heard all the noise! You're going to the king. I'm coming with you. I will tell the king … Um what must I tell the king?
CHICKEN LICKEN:	(puffing and panting) That the sky is falling down … some of it fell on my head …
HENNY PENNY:	… and we're all going to die.
FOXY LOXY:	(smiling) Hello everyone.
ALL:	(gabbling and making a big noise)
FOXY LOXY:	(looking serious) Hold on! I can't hear what you are saying if you all shout at once!
GANDER LANDER:	We're all going to die because the sky is falling down.
DRAKEY LAKEY:	So we need to go and tell the king.
FOXY LOXY:	(smirking) Ah! Now I understand. I know a quick way to get there. Follow me!

(They all set off behind the smirking FOXY LOXY.)

Scene 5: Outside and inside FOXY LOXY's dark underground den.

FOXY LOXY:	This way, hurry up … in you go!
GOOSEY LOOSEY:	Is this the king's castle? Doesn't look …
FOXY LOXY:	It's a short cut to the castle … come on! This way to the king … (Licking his lips as he looks at the others.)

(A little while later, FOXY LOXY and his family are eating.)

FOXY LOXY:	Hmm. That was good. I told them I'd take them to the king. I am the king!

4 Talk about the answers to the questions below.

a What did Chicken Licken think had happened at the beginning of the play?
b What really happened?
c Why did the other animals follow him?
d Where did Foxy Loxy lead the animals?
e What do you think Foxy Loxy planned to do?
f What do the words below from the play mean? Look for clues in the text.

> smirking   a den   fluffing up

g Some of the sentences and actions in the story are repeated. Do you think this makes the play funny? What else makes the play funny?
h What could the actors do to show the audience more about each character?

Word book
Remember to write interesting new words in your Word book.

Nouns and noun phrases

1 Copy the noun phrases below from the play. Circle the nouns and underline the adjectives. Do the adjectives go before or after the nouns?

- a big green acorn
- a dark underground den
- a quick way

Phrases
A phrase is a group of words without a verb. A noun phrase always has a noun and there are usually one or two adjectives that describe the noun. A noun phrase is more interesting than a noun on its own. For example:
- an old oak forest
- the excited animals.

2 Think about the animals in the play. Write your own noun phrases to describe the nouns below.

- Chicken Licken
- Foxy Loxy
- Turkey Lurkey

Writing

Write a paragraph to describe one of the characters from the play *Chicken Licken.* Look at the pictures and read what the character says. Use interesting adjectives and one or two noun phrases in your paragraph. Describe:

- what kind of animal it is.
- what it looks like.
- how it walks.

Reading and writing

1. Read the sentences below from the play aloud. Some of the words in the play have apostrophes because this matches the way we speak.

   a The sky's falling down!
   b You're in a hurry.
   c We're off to tell the king!
   d We'll all die if that happens.
   e I'm coming with you!

2. Write the sentences above. Write all the words in full.

3. Now read the sentences below. All the words are written in full. How would we say the underlined words when we speak?

   a <u>What is</u> going on?
   b <u>They are</u> going to tell the king that the sky is falling down.
   c I <u>cannot</u> hear what you are saying.
   d <u>It is</u> a short cut to the castle.
   e I told them <u>I would</u> take them to the king.

4. Write the sentences above using apostrophes to join the underlined words.

Reading aloud

GROUP WORK. Read the play *Chicken Licken* aloud in groups of eight.

- Think about the characters as you read.
- Add movement and gesture to help create the characters.
- Don't read the instructions aloud.
- You can make masks or other simple props to use.

Writing

1 PAIR WORK. Write a scene from a play based on the text from *Tiger Dead! Tiger Dead!* or any other traditional story that you know well.

Stories and plays

In a story, the writer of the story can explain what is happening.

In a play, the actors need to say what is happening and use gestures and actions to help the audience understand what is going on. The text in italic script gives the actors **instructions**.

STEP 1 Plan your scene
- Choose the characters.
- Make sure you know what the character looks like.
- Think about how the character walks and talks.
- Think about adjectives that would describe the character, for example: *nervous, proud, scary, fierce.*

STEP 2 Draft your scene
- Use a piece of paper.
- Describe the setting.
- Write the names of the characters on the left with colons. Look at the play *Chicken Licken* again.
- Write instructions for the actors. For example (*ANANSI walks into the house.*)
- Then write what the characters say to each other.
- Don't use speech marks (this is a playscript, not a story).
- Use short forms of words with apostrophes.

STEP 3 Read your draft scene aloud
- Does it sound right?
- Have you written an ending to the scene?

2. **Improve your playscript.**
   - Include a few instructions to the actors.
   - Can you use better synonyms instead of some of the words you have used?
   - Have you used long and short sentences?
   - Have you used the correct punctuation (apostrophes) in words that are in short form?

   STEP 4 Perform your play for the class.

Reading

1. Read the poem below silently. Make sure that you understand the poem.

2. **PAIR WORK.** Then practise reading the poem aloud with rhythm and expression.
   - How will you read the dialogue in the poem?
   - How will you read the words that are repeated in the poem?

The Stone Cutter
By Sean Taylor

A poor stone cutter
chipped at a rock.
His hammer went TACK
and his chisel went TOCK.

Then a rich man walked past,
in his rich man's clothes.
"I'm just a poor stone cutter,"

the stone cutter said.
"I'd rather be a rich man instead."

And he became a rich man.

Then the emperor rode past,
 with his servants dressed in blue and gold.
"I'm just a rich man," the stone cutter said.
"I'd rather be the emperor instead."

And he became the emperor.

Then the sun came out.
It was grander and more powerful
than any emperor.

"I'm just an emperor," the stone cutter said.
"I'd rather be the sun instead."

And he became the sun.

Then a big cloud passed.
It blocked out all the sun's light.
"I'm just the sun," the stone cutter said.
"I'd rather be a cloud instead."

And he became a cloud.

Then a wild wind blew the cloud
away across the sky.
"I'm just a cloud," the stone cutter said.
"I'd rather be the wind instead."

And he became the wind.

The wind blew until
it smacked into a huge rock.
"I'm just the wind," the stone cutter said.

"I'd rather be a rock instead."

And he became a rock.

Then he felt a poor stone cutter
chipping at his side.
"I'm just a rock," the stone cutter said.
"I'd rather be a poor stone cutter instead."

And he became a poor stone cutter once again.

A poor stone cutter
chipped at a rock.
His hammer went TACK
and his chisel went TOCK.

Vocabulary

Read the sentences below from the poem. Then answer the questions.

- Then a wild wind blew the cloud away across the sky.
- The wind blew until it smacked into a huge rock.
- His hammer went TACK and his chisel went TOCK.
- Then he felt a poor stone cutter chipping at his side.

a Which words in each sentence add a lot of meaning to the sentence?
b What do the words mean?
c Which words describe sounds?

Writing

Write a play about *The Stone Cutter*. Use the flowchart you made about the story in your Workbook to help you.

- Think about the characters. How would they move and speak?
- What props would you need?

Thinking time

- What did you enjoy about acting out a play?
- What is the difference between writing a play and writing a story?
- How can you express what you feel in a play?

8 Amazing ships

Reading

1 Read the contents page and the index from the book *The Titanic*. Answer the questions below.

a Is this a fiction or non-fiction book?
b What was special about the ship *Titanic*? (Use the contents to help you work this out.)
c How many chapters or main sections are there in this book?
d What can you read about on page 10?
e In which section will you find an explanation of what happened?
f On which pages could you find out more about lifeboats?
g Which list is organised in alphabetical order? Why?

The Titanic

Contents

The biggest ship ever 2
Maiden voyage 4
Life on board 6
Trouble ahead 8
Iceberg! 10
To the lifeboats! 12
The ship goes down 14
Help at last 16
What went wrong? 18
Under the sea 20
Glossary 21
Index 21
The voyage of the Titanic 22

Written by Anna Claybourne
Collins

Index

Carpathia, the   11, 16
first class   6, 7
iceberg   8, 9, 10
lifeboats   12, 13, 16, 19
lifejackets   15
maiden voyage   4
New York   4
Southampton   4
wreck   20

2 **PAIR WORK.** Read the text. Write any words that are not familiar. Then try to work out the meanings of the words.

The Titanic
by Anna Claybourne

The biggest ship ever
A new ship set sail over 100 years ago. Her name was *Titanic,* which means 'giant'. She was the biggest passenger boat ever built and could carry 3,500 people.

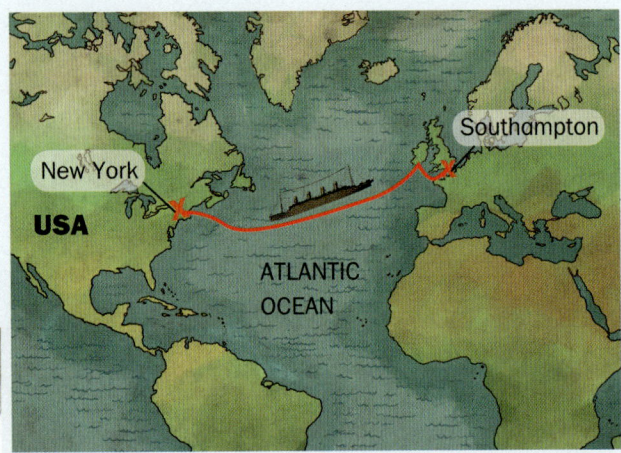

Life on board
First-class passengers had beautiful rooms, with carpets and **chandeliers**.

There were restaurants, lounges, steam baths, a library and a gym.

Maiden voyage
On 10 April 1912, the *Titanic* left Southampton, England, on her **maiden voyage**.

She was heading for New York, in the United States of America. Over 2,200 passengers and crew were making the six-day journey.

Trouble ahead

For four days, the *Titanic* steamed ahead, in calm, bright weather.

Then, late at night on 14 April, the **lookout** spotted something in the dark.

"Iceberg!" he shouted.

An iceberg is very dangerous for ships because most of the iceberg is under water and it cannot be seen.

To the lifeboats!

Sadly, the *Titanic* only had 20 lifeboats. There wasn't enough space for everyone. In the panic, only about 700 people got a place.

The ship goes down

Slowly, the *Titanic* began to **tilt**. Then she broke in two and at 2:20 a.m. on 15 April, she sank.

Many people fell into the icy water. Many of them had lifejackets, but couldn't survive in the freezing cold water for long.

Iceberg!

At 11:40 p.m. the *Titanic* scraped along the iceberg, making rips and cracks in her **hull**. Icy seawater flooded in. The *Titanic* was doomed.

Another ship, the *Carpathia*, heard the Titanic's **SOS** radio signal. She raced to help.

77

Help at last

The survivors waited in the lifeboats, shivering. Then at 4:00 a.m. a light shone in the darkness. It was the *Carpathia*.

Only 705 people were rescued. At least 1,500 died. On 18 April the *Carpathia* arrived in New York with the survivors.

What went wrong?

The *Titanic* disaster was one of the worst shipwrecks ever.

There weren't enough lifeboats because people thought this massive ship couldn't sink. They were wrong!

Under the sea

In 1985, explorers found the wreck of the *Titanic* on the seabed, 4 kilometres deep.

Glossary

chandelier: a large glass light with lots of bulbs
maiden voyage: a ship's first journey
hull: the outer wall of a ship
lookout: someone whose job is to watch for danger
SOS: an emergency signal in which the letters 'SOS' are spelt out
tilt: leaning too much one way

Reading and writing

Scan the text quickly to find facts to answer the questions below. Write your answers.

a What does the name *Titanic* mean?
b When did the *Titanic* make this voyage?
c From which port did she sail?
d What was her destination?
e At what time did the ship hit an iceberg?
f How long did it take for the ship to sink?
g Why did many people not get into lifeboats?
h How many people died?
i How many people survived?
j Which ship came to the rescue of the passengers?

Remember!

A **fact** is something we can check or prove, or something that really happened. Dates or times are facts.

An **opinion** is what someone thinks. For example, some people thought that the Titanic could not sink. It is a fact that the Titanic did sink.

Reading and writing

Make up a fact file about the *Titanic*. Use information from the text you have read. Make sure you use the correct vocabulary. Make up a chart with headings. For example:

Facts about the *Titanic*

Name	
Description of ship	
Journey	
Dates	
Passengers	
Sinking	

Remember!

You can also use the internet to research interesting facts about the *Titanic*. For example, find out where it was built, how many cabins there were and how long and heavy it was.

Vocabulary

PAIR WORK. Read the sentences below. Then answer the questions.

- The lookout on the ship <u>saw</u> something in the water.
- The side of the ship <u>touched</u> against the iceberg.
- The seawater <u>poured</u> into the ship through a hole.
- Most people believed that the <u>big</u> ship couldn't sink.
- Many people fell into the <u>cold</u> water and drowned.
- The *Carpathia* <u>sailed</u> quickly to rescue the survivors.

a Find the underlined words. Are they verbs or adjectives?

b Find verbs or adjectives in the text that express the same ideas, but in a more powerful or interesting way.

Word book

Record any interesting words in your Word book.

Punctuation

1 Rewrite the sentences below using capital letters, full stops, exclamation marks, question marks and speech marks.

a people thought that the titanic could not sink they were wrong
b what went wrong on the night of 14 april
c the lookout was standing on the deck when suddenly he shouted iceberg

2 Then read each sentence aloud. Look carefully at the punctuation as you read.

Using punctuation marks to read aloud

Full stop: pause

Question mark: your voice goes up

Exclamation mark: read louder

Speech marks: try to sound like a real person speaking

Spelling

1 Make compound words with the words in the box. You can use some words more than once. Write the words and learn to spell them.

> ice sea berg look wreck life
> boat water jacket out ship

2 Make adjectives and nouns with the words in the box. Use suffixes such as: –or, –er, –ed, –ment, –less. Check your spelling in a dictionary.

Examples:
sail → sailor   life → lifeless

> survive freeze bake inspect
> visit enjoy manage act
> photograph doom calm help

Speaking and writing

1 **GROUP WORK. Imagine you are all on the *Titanic*.** Some of you are passengers and others are people who work on the ship. Someone comes to tell you the ship has hit an iceberg. Talk about the questions below.

a What do you say?
b How do you feel?
c What do you do?

2 Write a short playscript based on the scene you have talked about.

- Make a list of the characters first. Include at least four passengers and two members of the crew. Think about each character. What would they do? Be calm and quiet? Shout and scream? Cry? Say nothing?
- Remember to describe the setting.
- Use words that have impact.
- Evaluate your play and improve it.

Scene: In the first-class lounge on the Titanic.
14 April 1912: Time: 11:45 p.m.

Mr _____ : What was that?

Miss _____ : I heard a loud scraping sound.

Mr _____ :

Ben (crew): Everyone up on deck – QUICKLY!

Speaking

Using body language

We can express feelings through words but we can also express meaning through our 'body language'. Look at the examples of the ways in which three people reacted to some news.

- Look at their faces.
- Look at what they have done with their hands.
- Look at the way they are standing or sitting.

1. **Look at the pictures below.**
   a What do you think each person may have heard or seen?
   b Describe their body language.

> **Prepositions**
>
> Prepositions are short words that we use before nouns to describe:
> - where someone or something is
> - what time or date it is
> - in which direction something or someone is going.

2. **GROUP WORK. Practise and perform the play scene you have written. Use body language to show how each character feels.**

Reading and writing

1. **Imagine you were on the *Titanic* and you survived the accident. Write a short report for a newspaper about what happened to you that night. Use information from the text you have read. Remember to link your sentences with words such as 'Before', 'Later', 'Then', 'After that'.**

2. **Now check your spelling.**
   - Make sure you have copied words from the text correctly.
   - Compound words are easy to spell. Break the words up into two words and spell each word.
   - Check verbs and plural noun forms. Have you used *–s*, *–ies*, *–es*, *–ing* and *–ed* correctly?

> **Remember!**
>
> We can vary the way we start sentences.
>
> <u>Then, slowly,</u> the *Titanic* began to sink. (This emphasises the <u>manner</u> in which the boat sank.)
>
> <u>At 2.20 a.m.,</u> the *Titanic* sank into the water. (This emphasises the <u>time</u> at which the boat sank.)
>
> <u>Far away from land, in the middle of the Atlantic,</u> the boat began to go down. (This emphasises the <u>place</u> where the ship sank.)

Reading and speaking

PAIR WORK. Look carefully at the picture below. Read all the labels. Talk about the answers to the questions.

a What is LNG?
b How is this ship different from the *Titanic*?
c Where is the LNG stored on this ship?
d Why does the ship have a thick hull?
e Where would you expect to find the captain of this ship?
f Why does the ship need a ballast tank?
g What do you think is the destination of this ship?

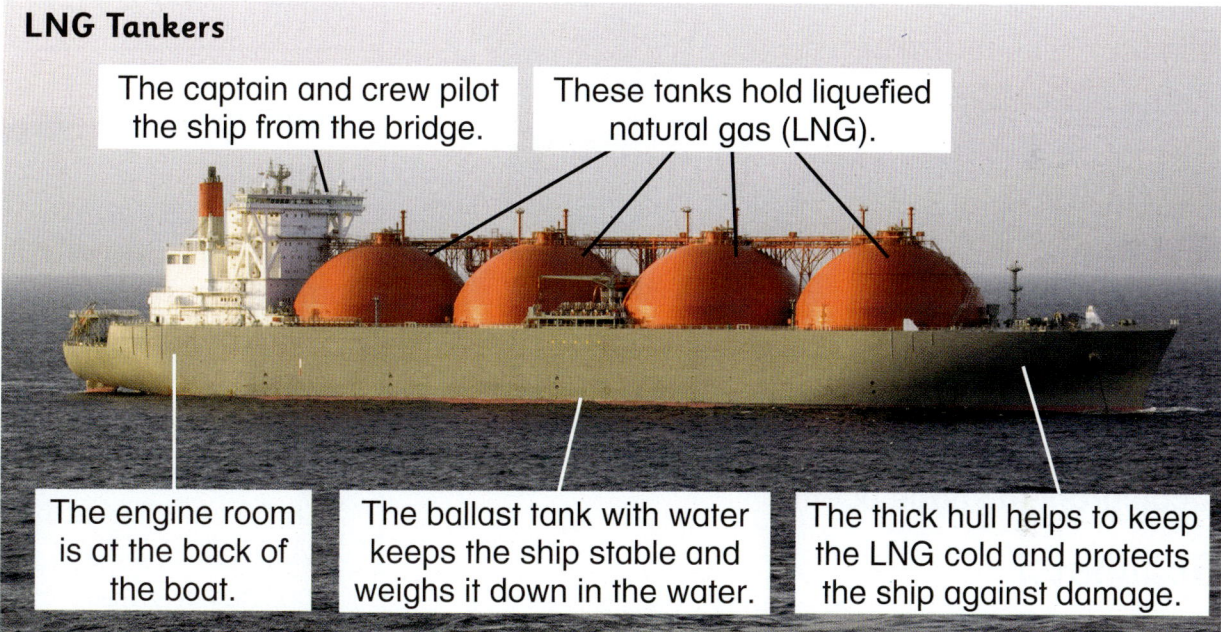

LNG Tankers

- The captain and crew pilot the ship from the bridge.
- These tanks hold liquefied natural gas (LNG).
- The engine room is at the back of the boat.
- The ballast tank with water keeps the ship stable and weighs it down in the water.
- The thick hull helps to keep the LNG cold and protects the ship against damage.

Vocabulary

Put the groups of words below from this unit in alphabetical order.

a hull tank iceberg voyage
b crew chandelier captain cold
c survivor scrape spot ship

Remember!

Remember that if two words begin with the same letter, you need to look at the second letter to decide which order to put the words in.

Thinking time

- How did you go about looking for facts about the *Titanic*?
- What can you do to check that your facts are correct?

83

9 Sights, sounds and feelings

Reading and speaking

1 GROUP WORK. Read the poems below aloud.

A limerick

There was a young girl from Goole,
Who took her pet snake to school.
   It squiggled and wriggled
   And the whole class giggled.
Her teacher didn't think it was cool.

Anonymous

A calligram (a shape poem)

Spaghetti

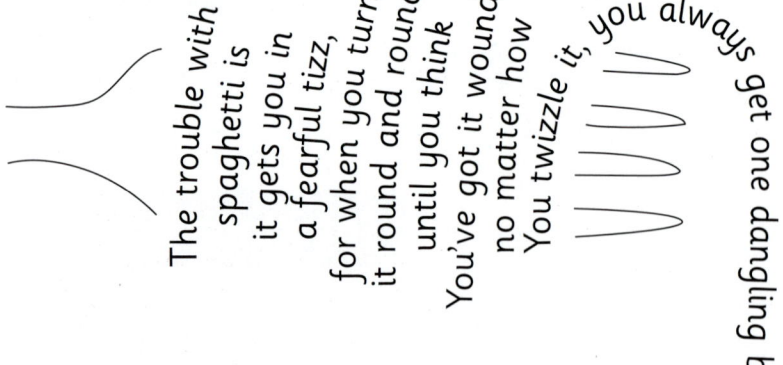

by Noel Petty

Poems
There are many different ways of writing poems. Some poets use patterns or shapes, others use rhyming words and rhythm.

Limericks
Limericks are nonsense poems. They all have the same pattern.
- There are always five lines.
- Lines 1, 2 and 5 have the same number of stressed syllables (or beats) and they rhyme.
- Lines 3 and 4 have the same number of stressed syllables (or beats) and they rhyme.

Calligrams
A **calligram** is a shape poem. The words in the poem are arranged in a shape or a picture.

An acrostic poem

> **Acrostic poems**
> Acrostic poems use the letters of a word or name. Each line of the poem starts with a letter from the name or word.

I am Indira

Intelligent
Never sad
Dutiful
Interesting
Reliable
Annoying sometimes!

2 Which poem do you like best? Why?
- Did it make you laugh?
- Did it make you think?
- Was it fun to read aloud?
- Which poems have words that rhyme?

Write a poem

1 Work with a partner or alone. Write a shape poem or a limerick or an acrostic poem.

2 Display your poem in class and read it aloud. Read with as much expression as possible. You want your classmates to enjoy the poems as much as you do!

Reading and listening

1 Listen and follow as your teacher reads the two poems on pages 85 and 86 by Judith Nicholls.

Riddle

I am
pear-drop
space-hopper
rest-on-a-tail:
fast as a rocket,
and what's in my pocket
small as a snail?
I'm shorter than elephant,
taller than man:
I hop-step-and jump
as no creature can.
My jacket is fur,
my pocket too;
a joey hides there …
I am
KANGAROO!

Teacher said …

You can use
  mumbled and muttered
  groaned, grumbled and uttered
  professed, droned or stuttered
    … but don't use SAID!

You can use
  rant or recite
  yell, yodel or snort
  bellow, murmur or moan
  you can use grunt or just groan
    … but don't use SAID!

You can use
  hum, howl and hail
  scream, screech, shriek or bawl
  squeak, snivel or squeal
  with a blood-curdling wail
    … but don't use SAID!
    … SAID my teacher.

Did you enjoy these poems by Judith Nicholls? She has written many other poems that you may enjoy. You can listen to some of her poems online.

2 GROUP WORK. Compare the poems. How do the poems work? Take roles in your group and report back to the class with your ideas.

- Is there a pattern to each poem?
- Find examples of words that rhyme.
- Find examples of words that have the same beginning sounds.
- Are there sentences with the same number of syllables?
- How many sections are there in each poem?
- Which poem did you enjoy most? Why?

Rhythm

Poets use special techniques to create rhythm in a poem. A poem with rhythm is more fun to read aloud and perform. Here are a few of the techniques:

- words that rhyme, have the same end sound ('hail', 'wail')
- words that start with the same sounds ('yell', 'yodel')
- sentences with the same number of syllables.

Vocabulary

1 Read *Riddle* again. Choose the best answers below.

a In this poem a 'space-hopper' means …
- something that can hop over spaces
- something that hops up in the sky.

b A kangaroo is an animal that …
- runs very slowly
- runs very fast.

c The kangaroo's 'jacket' is …
- its furry skin
- the pocket on the front of its body.

d A 'joey' is …
- the kangaroo's food
- a baby kangaroo.

2 PAIR WORK. Read *Teacher said* … again.

One person role-plays a word from the box.
The other person has to guess what the word is.

mumble	stutter	snort	murmur
squeal	snivel	grunt	mutter

Grammar and writing

1 PAIR WORK. Read *Teacher said* … again. Then answer the questions.

a Which verbs could you use instead of 'said' if you want to say that someone said something loudly?

b Which verbs could you use to describe someone talking softly or not clearly?

2 Think of more synonyms that you could use instead of 'said' and write another verse for the poem. Read your verse to the class.

Synonyms

Synonyms are words that have the same or a similar meaning. For example, 'giggle' and 'chuckle' are synonyms of 'laugh'.

Word book

Write interesting synonyms in your Word book.

3 Use *Teacher said* … as a pattern for your own poem with synonyms. You can use idea below. Then write another verse of your own.

> Teacher said …
> You can use
> left, departed, set off
> travelled and journeyed
> vanishes, disappeared or escaped
> … but don't use WENT!

Think of synonyms for 'walked' and 'laughed' and write more verses.

Write a riddle

1 PAIR WORK. Write riddles about other animals that you know. You need to give the reader some clues like the ones below.

- describe what the animal looks like
- describe how it moves
- mention some of the things it does
- say what it eats
- say where it lives

It is small and it moves slowly. It takes its house with it! It …

2 Read your riddles aloud to the class.

Listening and speaking

1 Close your eyes and listen as your teacher reads the poems on pages 89–91.

2 Talk about the poems.
- All the poems use words that add a lot of meaning to the poem. Give examples from each poem.
- Which poem made you laugh? Give a reason for your answer.
- Which poem appealed to your senses (made you feel, smell or hear something)?
- Which poem had the most rhythm? How did the poet create the rhythm?
- Which poems have sound words? Find five sound words and say the words aloud. Talk about how they help you understand the meanings of the words.

3 GROUP WORK. Choose one of the poems and read it aloud.

Ice Cream and Fizzy Lemonade

Ice cream is sliding, soft and cold
And gives a smooth and soothing coat
On hot summer days
To the back of your throat.

Fizzy lemonade looks like water
But as you unscrew the bottle top
Bubbles crowd together in froth
With a rushing sound and a sudden pop.

It prickles and tickles your nose
And tingles the back of your throat
That needs another sliding soft
   ice cream
To give it back a smooth and
   soothing coat.

By Stanley Cook

Night Songs

"Pung-la-la," from the frog by my window.
"Shirr-ooo-ooo," from the midnight manicou.
"Ba-lo-ma," from the agouti in the yard.
"Rill-dee-dee," from the mongoose in the tree.
"Gonck-gonck," from the tatou by the pole.
"Urol-el-el," from the matapel.
"Goodnight," I whisper to my moonlight friends
singing their bedtime songs to the sky.

By Lynn Joseph

Hurricane

Shut the windows
Bolt the doors
Big rain coming
Climbing up the mountain

Neighbours whisper
Dark clouds gather
Big rain coming
Climbing up the mountain

Gather in the clothes lines
Pull down the blinds
Big wind rising
Coming up the mountain

Branches falling
Raindrops flying
Treetops swaying
People running
Big wind blowing
Hurricane! on the mountain

By Dionne Brand

4 **PAIR WORK. Listen to your teacher read *Night Songs*. Then write a poem with sound effects. Your poem can be about something that makes a particular noise or sound: a vacuum cleaner, the wind, an animal. Try to write words that sound like the sounds. Read your poem aloud to your class.**

Fishes' Evening Song

Flip flop,
Flip flap,
Slip slap,
Lip lap;
Water sounds,
Soothing sounds.
We fan our fins
As we lie
Resting here
Eye to eye.
Water falls
Drop by drop,
Plip plop,
Drip drop.
Plink plunk,
Splash, splish;
Fish fins fan,
Fish tails swish,
Swush, swash, swish
This we wish …
Water cold,
Water clear,
Water smooth,
Just to soothe
Sleepy fish.

By Dahlov Ipcar

The Hen

The hen is a ferocious fowl.
She pecks you till she makes you howl.

And all the time she flaps her wings,
And says the most insulting things.

And when you try to take her eggs,
She bites large pieces from your legs.

The only safe way to get these,
Is to creep up on your hands and knees.

In the meanwhile a friend must hide,
And jump out on the other side.

And then you snatch the eggs and run,
While she pursues the other one.

The difficulty is, to find
A trusty friend who will not mind.

By Lord Alfred Douglas

Remember!

Poets sometimes make up words to echo the sounds of things in poems. They also start pairs of words with the same letter or use rhyming words to create sounds.

Vocabulary

1 Write five interesting words from the poems you have listened to.

2 Say if your words are nouns, adjectives or verbs.

3 Then make your own sentence with each verb.

Word	Noun, adjective or verb	My sentences

If you enjoyed these poems, here are the names of some other poets you may enjoy:
John Agard
Grace Nichols
Roger McGough
Michael Rosen
Kenn Nesbitt
Judith Nicholls

Reading and speaking

Choose the poem that you like best from the poems you have listened to and talked about. Make sure you understand it first. Learn it and read it aloud. You can add actions as well.

How to read a poem aloud

- Make sure you understand and can say all the words in the poem. Make sure you know which words rhyme!
- Make a copy of the poem and use a pencil to mark the words you want to stand out.
- Look at the punctuation in the poem. Pause after commas and full stops. Raise your voice for exclamation marks.
- Think about the meaning of the poem and how you should read it. Should you sound serious, amused, bored or scared?

Thinking time

- Choose one poem you enjoyed the most. Think about what you liked about it. Share your ideas with the class.
- Why do you think you enjoyed some poems more than others?